Praise for
Hot Chocolate for Couples

Hot Chocolate for Couples is packed with some of my favorite things: chocolate, ideas for conversations with my husband that taste better than chocolate, and the "hot chocolate," red-hot monogamy moments that might follow. It overflows with humor, real-life illustrations, positive and workable insights, and nuggets of advice that will make your marriage even sweeter than chocolate.

—PAM FARREL, RELATIONSHIP EXPERT AND AUTHOR OF
MEN ARE LIKE WAFFLES, WOMEN ARE LIKE SPAGHETTI
AND *RED-HOT MONOGAMY*

I devoured *Hot Chocolate for Couples*. In fact, I enjoyed it so much I gained two pounds reading it! I know you'll love it too. A combination of serious fun and practical resources, this book is a must for every wedding shower, every counseling office bookshelf, and every married couple's bedside.

—DR. KEVIN LEMAN, AUTHOR OF
SHEET MUSIC AND *SEX BEGINS IN THE KITCHEN*

A sweet surprise! Cindy Sigler Dagnan offers up a recipe to last a lifetime!

—CYNDY SALZMANN, AUTHOR OF THE
FRIDAY AFTERNOON CLUB MYSTERY SERIES

Whether speaking boldly to thousands or sharing intimately through her books, Cindy's heart and wisdom are always vibrantly evident. Equally humorous and practical, fresh and timeless—Cindy has done it again with *Hot Chocolate for Couples*. In 25 years of counseling thousands of couples, every marriage we've seen would've been blessed by this hilarious guide to deeper love. This is the book you give to the new bride, your sister, your dearest friend, and yourself.

—DR. KARL AND SHANNON WENDT,
HOSTS OF *HOUSE CALLS*, AUTHORS OF *HOW TO
TALK TO YOUR KIDS ABOUT SEX*

This *must* be a good book. After reading it, I immediately wanted to give my wife a big hug, plan a surprise date, and do the laundry.

—Dr. Todd Cartmell, Psy.D., author of *Respectful Kids* and *Keep the Siblings, Lose the Rivalry*

Cindy Dagnan has crafted a marriage manual that is the perfect blend of practical and profound, of both lighthearted anecdotes and loving advice. Its chapters serve as wisdom-filled, yet witty and whimsical guides ready to point wives in the right and God-honoring direction. Her chocolate-cloaked counsel will encourage you to live a life that accurately reflects a strikingly beautiful picture of Christ and the church.

—Karen Ehman, national speaker for Proverbs 31 Ministries and Hearts at Home, author of *A Life That Says Welcome*

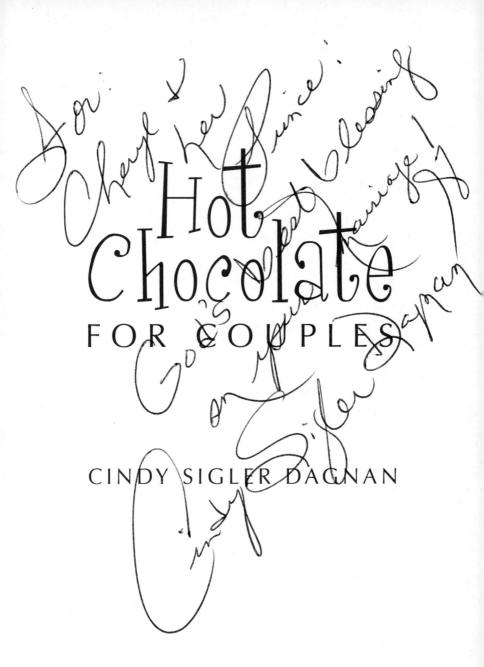

Hot Chocolate

FOR COUPLES

CINDY SIGLER DAGNAN

HARVEST HOUSE PUBLISHERS

EUGENE, OREGON

Cover photos © Fanelie Rosier / iStockphoto; Jill Fromer / iStockphoto

Cover by Dugan Design Group, Bloomington, Minnesota

Published in association with the literary agency of WordServe Literary Group, Ltd., 10152 S. Knoll Circle, Highlands Ranch, CO 80130

HOT CHOCOLATE FOR COUPLES
Formerly *Chocolate Kisses for Couples*
Copyright © 2007 by Cindy Sigler Dagnan
Published by Harvest House Publishers
Eugene, Oregon 97402
www.harvesthousepublishers.com

978-0-7369-2729-1

Library of Congress Cataloging-in-Publication Data
   Dagnan, Cindy Sigler.
   [Chocolate kisses for couples]
   Hot chocolate for couples / Cindy Sigler Dagnan.
      p. cm.
   Includes bibliographical references.
   ISBN 978-0-7369-2729-1 (pbk.)
   1. Spouses—Religious life. 2. Marriage—Religious aspects—Christianity. I. Title.
   BV4596.M3D34 2009
   248.8'44—dc22

                                  2008055424

Printed in the United States of America

         09 10 11 12 13 14 15 / VP-SK / 11 10 9 8 7 6 5 4 3 2 1

Acknowledgments

Thanks to my awesome prayer team for this book: Patsy, Emmy, Ellie, Angie, Vickie, Sharris, Ginny, Debbie, Karen, Cheryl, Reggie "Favorite," and Sherm. It is the most humbling and thrilling feeling to know that those who love you are carrying you before the throne.

Thanks to my agent, Greg Johnson, and to Becky, who totally "get" my chocolate heart.

Thanks to Hope Lyda—I pray you are forever my editor. You crack me up. I'll send you red throw pillows for your couch manuscript and puff ball socks to boot!

Thanks to John Hunter, research librarian at Ozark Christian College, and to Sherm Nichols who let me badger him with questions about witness piles and covenants.

Thanks to Rusty R. and Mike (leave the plants alone!) L. and all the rest of Webb City's finest; Brian Leeper—here you go!; Aaron Houk and the other illustrious firefighters; our VHCC family; Sue Utter and all those who returned surveys.

For my accountability group—you make everything fun, even FBC. I pray we reach the finish line together.

Thanks to Will and Jill Blaylock and the small but mighty Thursday morning Bible study group.

Thanks to my awesome group of "Rough Draft Readers," including a former student who nowadays gets to grade her teacher's papers.

Especially warm thanks to Marguerite, Dorothy, and Vi. From your combined total of more than a century and a half of marriage, I have gleaned treasure upon treasure with which to polish my own marriage. You girls are still fabulous! I hope God plays the recording of you in your "short britches" and "weird lipstick and nail polish" so I can watch it with you in heaven.

My four precious blessings: Eden, Emmy, Ellie and Elexa. The highlight of my nights is tucking you in. There aren't words enough to describe how much I love you. Eden, keep running, but always for Jesus. When He is your finish line, you will always make the Big Time! Emmy, I look forward to reading the work of the next writer in the family—hang on to that series idea; you amaze me. Ellie, from basketball games to grins and compassion, Boppa would be proud. Daddy and I sure are. Elexa, if Daddy and I could have hand-picked our "caboose," we couldn't have done any better. Girls, we are so glad that God chose us to be your parents! If we do nothing else right, we hope to point you to God and leave you the legacy of a "forever family." "So do not throw away your confidence, it will be richly rewarded" (Hebrews 10:35).

My faithful heavenly Father, thank You for graciously wrestling me to the ground on this one; I beg You not to let go until You bless me. I know I have so much more to learn; thanks for loving me, mess that I am. That You have given me the desires of my heart astounds me still!

Contents

The Whole Box of Chocolates:
Each Piece an Adventure 9

1 Crazy Little Thing Called a Honeymoon:
New Love 15

2 What Lies Beneath:
Expectations and Reality 33

3 The Sweetness of Covenant:
Forgiveness and Promises 51

4 Communicating in Chocolate:
Breaking the Code 71

5 Sharing Chocolate:
Doing Life Together 87

6 Chocolate Drops:
When Children Come Along 109

7 Better Than Chocolate:
Sexual Intimacy 131

8 Unwrapping Love's Delights:
Setting the Mood 145

9 Protecting Your Chocolate:
Boundaries for a Healthy Marriage 163

10 Captivated by Chocolate:
What You Love Most 185

11 Chocolate Glue:
A Made to Last Marriage 205

Conversation Starters for Married Couples 223

Hot Chocolate Surveys 225

Notes 231

A Love Like This

CINDY SIGLER DAGNAN

Bridal lace, yellowed with age
Black and white photographs,
Certain memories of another day.

Thirty-three years together,
Sweat, toil, and tear stains,
Struggles, triumphs.

Two little girls, now grown.
A love alone,
Saddled with cancer; riddled with doubt
Determined to conquer.

Love that will honor
Vows spoken in another time;
Promises for better or worse.
In sickness and in health

Uttered on another day when
Such words seemed a mockery of life.

This day, they know better,
Yet they will cling to that love
Even more tenaciously at death's door.

Preciousness will follow this walk into Eternity;
This is what we seek,
A Love like This.

The Whole Box of Chocolates
Each Piece an Adventure

This book is fun, it's accurate, it's user-friendly, and if I did my job listening to God as I wrote, it can change the outlook of a marriage. But this has been a hard book to write because, even with the humor, this is a book of hard stuff. I didn't *really* want to do a no-spin, tell-it-like-it-is job. I wanted lots of laughs combined with tender, amusing anecdotes (the hallmark of my books) to provide the humorous window into my family life. But as I started writing, my wonderful husband and I began, and are still doing, some of the hardest work of our married life, and Satan didn't want us to succeed.

If there is one thing Satan really wants to destroy, to use for evil, and to help ruin the cause of Christ, it's our families. There's no better place for him to begin than with marriage because it has always been the bedrock of society. He'll use any methods—the stupid, the insidious, the grand, and the tawdry. He'll go from the deadly serious to the innocuous. I've seen examples of both during the timeline of this book.

One evening I had been invited to speak to some children about the writing process. There was a brief song service and devotional time before the people broke into various small group studies and children's activities. At the end of the gathering time, a precious man stepped forward to the microphone. While I think we all were expecting a simple announcement, what we witnessed was an incredible, repentant act of humble courage. This man explained to the congregation that he'd already asked for forgiveness from his wife, his children, and the church elders for sinning against his wife, but he felt he needed to confess to his church family, ask for their forgiveness, and request that they help hold him accountable.

My heart broke for this man and his family, and I prayed for them. It's not the only story I've witnessed, old or new. It was just a variation on Satan's endless, favorite theme: unfaithfulness. Unfaithfulness can take shape in many forms and on many different levels. Sometimes we are unfaithful by investing our emotions in someone other than our spouse. But sometimes we are unfaithful in our motives or our intentions. We lose sight of the most important aspects of a relationship and let it fend for itself while we go about our activities. Sometimes we embrace the fatigue more than we embrace our mate. Frequently we fail to recognize our own needs that are left ignored or shortchanged for so long that we forget how to feel or be ourselves.

Satan certainly isn't above using me for an example under the heading "Stupid, Hypocritical Things to Do While Writing a Book on Marriage." In fact one evening when the children were settled, and our oldest was at home and, therefore, available to rescue the younger ones should the house catch fire, my husband announced that he'd like some ice cream. I handed him the remains of a Shake's Frozen Custard gift card from Christmas and tried to wave him out the door.

He looked crestfallen. "I was hoping you could go with me!"

I am ashamed to admit that I looked at him incredulously and announced, "You've got to be *kidding* me! You want me to go with you to get something I can't even *have?*" Didn't he know that I'd almost lost the last 15 post-baby pounds (after three years, mind you)? "You want me to go when I have a writing deadline?!!!" (Pardon the extra punctuation, but I need you to get the tone.)

Immediately I wished I could take the words back; clearly he just wanted a few moments of my company without the band of adorable, but relentless, ruffians that usually accompany us. But I couldn't take them back, and the moment passed. He drove to the McDonald's drive-through for a quick cone—alone. And I sat miserably at the computer, probably typing something about being in tune with your husband's needs.

Thankfully, if you're holding this book in your hand, together we can read, study, practice, and encourage each other not to pass up many more such opportunities.

I have used chocolate as both a theme and a metaphor for this book because it is, for the most part, an anticipated, pleasing thing. Still, chocolate serves as a tasty coating for the hard places in marriage, as a buffer against the wear and tear of the mundane and daily. Chocolate as a dessert represents a sweet benediction to the substance that makes up the marriage meal: talking, laughing, crying, praying, struggling, and persevering together.

Chocolate is the delight of sweet words on the tongue. When we want to shout out angry words or quitting words like "that's it," "I've had all I can take," or "I want out," the goodness of silence will serve us better. The expression of forgiveness and grace will enrich us and our spouse. We learn that the sweetness often comes after slogging through the bitter.

It is my prayer, and oh, how I have prayed for each of you during the research and writing of this book, that your marriage won't just survive, but it will thrive and then burst into blooms more glorious than anything you have ever imagined! It's my further prayer that this will happen because you are reaching for the sunshine of Him who is able to do exceedingly beyond all that we ask or dream. Doesn't the wonder of it all just steal your breath?

How to Use This Book

Well, I hope you don't put this down and flee the bookstore because you're wondering what kind of a wacko would write a section about how to use a book. Of course you *read* it! Or at least put it on the pile with the other things-I'll-get-around-to-doing.

Hang in there and give me a chance. Please. Depending on whose statistics you read, between 75 and 85 percent of all books are purchased by women, including those that are for men..."Oh, hey! I bet my husband would really enjoy reading this!" In this case, it is a book for both of you.

What that means is, unless you received this book as a gift from an extraordinarily thoughtful spouse, you probably bought it after browsing through the marriage section at your local bookstore. Leafing through the pages, you caught the spirit of fun and practicality within, started drooling over the thought of chocolate, and had to buy it. You envisioned sharing love, laughter, and the anointing winds of fresh change in your marriage. Perhaps, you're as naive as I once was, thinking that you'll just lay this book on your husband's pillow and he'll be enthralled. Purely on your recommendation, he'll pick it up, plow through the pages, and apply every principle that could possibly enhance his role as husband. And maybe he will.

Here's an alternate and more likely best-case scenario: You begin applying some of the principles in chapters seven and eight and he's intrigued. He leafs through the book, zeroing in on physical intimacy and deems this a winner. I'll get many grateful emails from husbands who are thankful that their wives have an in-print girlfriend who will truly talk about anything, including what our mates so desperately need. One of the women who proofread the chapter on physical intimacy had it "stolen" by her husband who read it and returned it marked with an A+ in the margin next to all of her comments.

And for the rest of us, here's how to use this book. Read it through at the pace of one chapter a week. Choose one thing to really pray about and begin applying it to your marriage. In each chapter there's a super short or humorous section to share with your husband. Read it to him while you're snuggled up in bed or hand it to him and ask him to please "read this part"!

At night or during your dinner date, use the "Hot Chocolate Topic," found at the end of each chapter, as a conversational springboard. Speaking of those, there's a list of "Conversation Starters for Married Couples" at the end of this book. Before the evening's over, consider delivering each chapter's "Goodnight Kiss."

Also, at the end of each chapter there are pertinent (and guy-approved) study questions. It's always great to blame the book or the author when bringing up a topic you've been avoiding for years! Seriously, allow time in the evening, during devotions, on dates, or on a retreat for the two of you to really share the answers to these questions with each other. Pray together. Be prepared to stretch, to grow, to be uncomfortable, and then, I pray, to fall in love with each other all over again.

Homemade Hot Chocolate

8 quarts powdered milk

1 pound Nestle Quick

1½ cups powdered sugar

4 tablespoons cocoa

7 ounces Coffeemate

Mix all ingredients in large bowl;
store in airtight container.

Add ½ cup mix to very hot water.

(This recipe is from Linda Campbell, a long-time married champion from Villa Heights Christian Church)

Crazy Little Thing
Called a Honeymoon
New Love

*I have now come to the conclusion never again to think
of marrying, and for this reason: I can never be satisfied with
anyone who would be blockhead enough to have me.*

ABRAHAM LINCOLN, IN A LETTER TO
MRS. ORVILLE BROWNING, APRIL 1, 1938[1]

I've got some pretty sad news for you. Good marriages take work. Heck, *all* marriages take work! Well, that's a double-rats statement for us girls who were raised on fairy tales, cut our teeth on our mothers' tame-compared-to-today's-fare paperback Harlequins, and slid into adolescence sneaking Saturday night glimpses of the oh-so-romantic *Love Boat*. If you're too young to have even seen that show on reruns, I don't want to hear about it. But trust me, it was a romantic playground come to life...or to television at least.

Most of us have dreamed of our wedding day, acted it out in dress-up with reluctant little brothers or unsuspecting guests, and browsed through countless issues of *Bride* magazine—all before we're even of an age or in a position to acquire married status.

In a family psychology class during my senior year of high school, we were required to make a wedding book. Page one had to list ten qualifications we were looking for in a mate. Then, in my idealistic opinion, we got to work on the "good stuff." Choosing a dress. Shoes. A color scheme. Invitations. A guest list. Rings. Flowers. And a flower girl. Ahhh! A cake. Reception site, food, decorations, and, to dance or not to dance? There was a little bit of naive giggling about the post-ceremony festivities—whether or not we just wanted to go straight to a hotel. But most of the honeymoon talk among my girlfriends was about two things: the location (we favored sun-drenched beaches with spectacular sunsets over emerald waves) and our trousseau. A going-away suit. Darling little short sets. Strappy sandals. One stunning swimsuit. Colorful, elegant sundresses. Evening gowns. And oh, yes, the lingerie. Impossibly fluffy gown and robe sets in every bridal shade from antique white to the palest seashell pink.

We gave little thought to what followed and absolutely *no* thought to how our attitudes, experiences, stereotypes, and role perceptions would affect our marriages.

Picture this. A 29-year-old woman is on her much-anticipated honeymoon in Cancun, Mexico. Everything is exquisite. Silky smooth marble floors. The choice of room service or a shamefully opulent buffet. A gigantic bed piled high with pillows, made up with crisp cotton sheets and a colorful spread. Warm ocean breezes push back sheer white panels. You can hear the slap of turquoise waves tickling white sand beaches. The view is something straight out of a travel poster.

She gets up before her new husband and scurries to the bathroom. She brushes her teeth and hair, then climbs back under the covers to pretend that she is the only woman in the world who wakes up without morning breath or bed head. By day three, she is exhausted and tired of the charade. She decides to chance it. Guess what? He loves her anyway! Sigh of relief.

Now rewind your mind's imagination tape about four years prior to this scene in paradise. A devastated young wife and mother cries in a tiny Midwestern apartment. She has taught school all day and driven home in a borrowed car. She opens the door to an empty apartment and immediately her eyes land on an envelope containing a note and two one-hundred dollar bills. Her husband has resigned his church and made clear his intentions to resign his marriage and abdicate his role as father of their sixteen-month-old daughter. Later she will discover that her car is gone and both savings and checking accounts are cleared out, except for the $1 mandated by the law in that state.

For the next three-and-half years, it will be just the young woman and her daughter. When they do regain some semblance of equilibrium and begin a contented, if vastly different, life than the young mother had dreamed for her family, she vows that she will never again be that vulnerable.

But God sometimes has different plans. A handsome detective on the Joplin Police force is assigned to work juvenile crime at the high school for part of each day. He speaks to the young woman's classes with wit and knowledge about search and seizure and due process. It doesn't hurt that he's good looking either. She is impressed, but determined to keep her distance. That conviction doesn't last long.

After several months of dating, it is obvious that the nature of their relationship will change. The love of her life gets down on one knee and actually does a magic trick—he swaps a bubble gum ring for a diamond solitaire and proposes. He promises to show her how the trick was done on their fiftieth wedding anniversary, thereby insuring they would be together always

You guessed it; both of the stories are mine. Beauty for ashes and the harvest of post-locust years, but not necessarily an easy happily ever after.

Bittersweet Expectations

Maybe we didn't come into marriage with the purity we had hoped. Or maybe we did, but felt it was wasted on the person for whom we'd waited. Like tin cans tied on the getaway car, bumping along under the shaving cream proclamation "JUST MARRIED," our scars, our expectations, our broken experiences, and our past mistakes will clamor along with us to the honeymoon and beyond.

If statistics are any indication, the current generation isn't getting a very positive picture of marriage. Why? "Adultescents (adults according to age, but with attitudes ten to twenty years younger, often irresponsible, and still living at home with mom and dad), having lived through decades of divorce and broken homes, have a low view of traditional family. They are committed instead to their "tribe," a community of friends that provides support with a minimum of commitment. A tribe is easier to maintain than a family, and it's much more "fun."[2]

Interestingly enough, cohabitating in order to "try marriage on" before committing doesn't shake off any of the disillusionment. Studies show that infidelity and divorce rates are even higher among couples who have lived together first. And three-quarters of cohabitating parents break up before their child's sixteenth birthday.[3] Cohabitation might be easier to dissolve, but it offers absolutely no protection against heartbreak.

Perhaps, if we've married for a wrong reason, such as to escape a bad situation or bad relationship or to fulfill our romantic dreams without a foundation in reality, we become disillusioned and full of doubts. *Doesn't he love me anymore? Did he ever love me enough? Maybe I should look for someone else.*

It is natural to have a driving desire to be loved and accepted; God created us that way. It *isn't* natural or realistic to pin all our hopes for that love on one person. Why? He is only a person. Though made in God's image, our husbands will never be able to fill the God-shaped hole inside each of us. They weren't meant to. Beth Moore writes:

> We each have our unmet needs, and we carry them around all day long like an empty cup. In one way or another, we hold out that empty cup to the people in our lives and say, "Can somebody please fill this? Even a tablespoon would help!"
>
> Whether we seek to have our cup filled through approval, affirmation, control, success, or immediate gratification, we are miserable until something is in it...No one is more

pleasurable to be around than a person who has had her cup filled by the Lord Jesus Christ. He is the only One who is never overwhelmed by the depth and *length* of our need.[4]

Moore goes on to explain that if we were to seek this from God each morning, every other person who poured into our little cups would just be joyous splashes of overflow! Imagine the freedom your husband would feel—God is more than enough! Imagine the freedom you could feel—it's no longer entirely your job to meet all of your husband's needs because God will do that!

Despite the questionable ethics in the popular movie *Jerry Maguire,* one of the romantic lines became a catch phrase: "You complete me." Our breath catches; we sigh in appreciation, and we long for that to be true of our relationships. And it *is* possible if we accept that complementing (not complimenting, although that's important too) each other means that we adopt different God-ordained roles. Early on in their marriage, Dr. Phil McGraw said that he and his wife, Robin, made a deal. She said, "You make the living, and I'll make the living worthwhile." With God in the midst, that is a worthy goal.

In a good, solid marriage, we have a preview of heaven. A blurry snapshot of God's love for us, His bride. To develop this picture, our marriage must be our number one earthly priority. Marriage expert Kevin Leman says, "If marriage is not the most important priority in your life, you are *never* going to have a real marriage, a marriage that includes commitment, that is full and satisfying emotionally, sexually, and spiritually."[5]

It's astonishingly easy for us to let that commitment slide and pick apart our relationships, replacing what we know to be true with shadowy apparitions of "if only," "what if," and "probably not." If our husband is late coming home, well then, he is inconsiderate and doesn't care about our feelings. If he tells us that an item we desperately want is not in the budget, well then, he certainly doesn't care about our happiness! If he has the audacity to disagree with us on an issue about which we feel passionately, we begin to reason that perhaps this isn't going to work out after all. We work hard at keeping up appearances, exhausting ourselves by trying to be perpetually perky and endlessly enigmatic.

Okay, confession time. For three *entire* months, if Greg was at home I turned the water faucet on when I had to pee. He finally said, "Hey, I know what you're doing in there!" We want to have it all, do it all, and be it all! How can we trust that someone could love us exactly the way we are?

Paul and Sandy Coughlin have a clever acronym for this kind of fear.

False

Evidence that

Appears

Real

Feelings aren't facts and we'll get in big trouble confusing the two.[6]

The Heart Work of Love

If we didn't grow up with the privilege of observing a godly, committed marriage and don't later get our hands on a solid blueprint of how it's supposed to look with wise premarital counseling, it seems logical to second guess our hearts.

> The life of the heart is a place of great mystery...We describe a person without compassion as "heartless," and we urge him or her to "have a heart." Our deepest hurts we call "heartaches." Jilted lovers are "brokenhearted." Courageous soldiers are "bravehearted." The truly evil are "black-hearted" and saints have "hearts of gold." If we need to speak at the most intimate level, we ask for a "heart-to-heart" talk. "Lighthearted" is how we feel on vacation. And when we love someone as truly as we may, we love "with all our heart." But when we lose our passion for life, when a deadness sets

in which we cannot seem to shake, we confess, "my heart's just not in it."[7]

As romantic as it sounds, the one thing I know we cannot trust is our hearts. We can't always "follow our hearts." Scripture tells us that "the heart is deceitful above all." We can be fooled.

Proverbs 4:23 also cautions "Above all else, guard your heart, for it is the wellspring of life." The Message translates it with even more bite: "Keep vigilant watch over your heart, that's where life starts."

Someone once said, "To love is to admire with the heart." Most of our men would be thrilled to feel our sincere admiration of who they are and what they do or try to do for us. It's just that lots of us don't have a clue what to do when the honeymoon bags are unpacked and the hard work of marriage begins.

When Greg and I were dating, we foolishly made what I always think of as the "kitchen cabinet promise." We declared to one another that we would not let our marriage sink to the abysmal depths that we observed around us. Our marriage would be different. Our late night marathon talks about life, dreams, memories, and philosophy would never stop. Our fights would be miniscule, our romantic aspirations over the top. Nothing, neither children, nor bills, nor adversity, nor petty irritations, would ever shake what we felt, what we had at this moment. Good grief! You'd have thought we were making a political speech!

We had no business making such a promise. Not because it wasn't admirable or romantic, but because we were leveling the pressure of filling a God-sized hole with another human being. We were setting ourselves up for disappointment.

What you're actually saying "I do" to is hard work! "The marriage ceremony isn't like graduation; rather, it's similar to the first day of kindergarten! It's not the culmination, but the beginning."[8] We need to start treating it that way.

A man and a woman were in their early thirties when they finally discovered each other and were married. They were in an elated state of anticipation on their honeymoon, except for one secret each had kept from the other: He had the stinkiest feet in the free world and she, the worst breath.

On their wedding night, while his bride was in the bathroom preparing herself, the groom undressed and slid all the way down under the blankets, praying that the covers would hide the smell of his feet while he waited for his bride.

Meanwhile, the bride procrastinated—brushing and flossing, gargling with mouthwash, and brushing again. Figuring that she couldn't put it off forever, she emerged from the bathroom. The eager groom patted the side of the bed.

Snuggled up beside him, the teary-eyed bride announced, "Oh, honey, I have something awful to tell you!"

"I think I know," the groom blurted out. "You ate my socks!"

Thankfully, not all of our honeymoon surprises are this bad! Still all of us have some surprise in store and some adjustments to make.

Checklist for Recapturing the Honeymoon

- ♥ If possible, return to the scene of your first date or the site of your proposal.

- ♥ Cuddle up with your favorite snacks and watch your wedding video.

- ♥ Shoot for a not-too-far-off anniversary and plan a spectacular celebration—a vow renewal ceremony, revisiting the church or city hall where your ceremony took place, a special trip.

- ♥ Let him open the door for you.

- ♥ Occasionally meet him at the door with his favorite beverage.

- ♥ Hold hands as you drift off to sleep.

- ♥ Cuddle on the couch.

- ♥ Read the Song of Solomon together. Out loud, if possible.

- ♥ Get a triple frame and choose your favorite courtship, wedding, and honeymoon photos to display.

- ♥ Go on a honeymoon "walk," verbally revisiting anniversary memories for each year.

- ♥ If the special nightgown you wore on your first night together still fits, get it out and wear it. If not, search for a similar one and spend a night away rekindling that feeling.

Someone Else to Think About

I met the charming Mrs. Wilma Davison at a women's luncheon where I spoke on a beautiful fall day in the Ozarks. I was privileged to be seated at her table and noticed that everyone was coming to her with their get-acquainted scavenger-hunt sheets in hand. They would ask, "Could you please sign here?" then they would point to the line that states, "Find someone who's been married more than 60 years."

I was intrigued. She had been married for 62 years. Her true love had been overseas, fighting in World War II. He proposed and sent the engagement ring to her via the mail! Her grandmother put the ring on her finger, and she waited until he returned.

"My next book is a marriage book," I shared and promptly peppered her with questions. "How did you meet your husband? How did you know he was the one?" She was delightful, transparent, warm, and real.

"What was the biggest adjustment that you faced when you were first married?" I queried. Her silver hair complemented perfect lipstick and a still fashionable style. She grinned, "Oh that's easy! It was remembering that there was someone besides me to think about!" We laughed together, for isn't that the truth?

If we're honest, most of us would admit that while we may have worked harder at this during courtship, frankly now that we're in the groove, we'd like for things to go our own way. If we're cold, the heat should be turned up. If we like lots of blankets, we should have them. If we're hot, well then, suddenly the expense of using the air conditioner is not quite as important as we'd claimed. We'd like to dine at our favorite restaurants and have him always remember to open our door. We'd like for this sort of behavior to continue whether or not we remember (or find it convenient) to hold up our end.

I get tickled with my oldest daughter. She wants a pink kitchen and is delighted at the catalog pictures of pink toasters, mixers, coffee makers, and irons. "What if your husband, um, doesn't want a pink kitchen?" I asked her one day.

"Well, I just can't get married then, Mom. I want someone manly enough not to mind a pink kitchen and who'll let me cook only the things that I like and, oh yeah, I want to be home every Christmas. I don't want to have to go to his family's." A perfectly idealistic, freshly turned sixteen answer.

Her daddy snorted. "Let us know how that works for you!"

I suggested that perhaps she'd better narrow her plan to include dating orphans only; she thought that might be a grand idea! Although we were all teasing, at the heart was an issue that hurts many a marriage—selfishness.

This insidious little weed has its roots in us from the moment we are born. We wail lustily when life is not going our way. Among our first words as toddlers are "No!" and "Mine!" Our self-centeredness often prevents us from making the smallest of compromises once the shades begin to lower, blocking out the honeymoon glow.

In the Bible, the Song of Solomon 2:15 reads, "Catch for us the foxes, the little foxes that ruin the vineyards, our vineyards that are in bloom." What might be the little foxes in our own lives that put our harvest at risk when they are ready to bear fruit? Pride. Self-centeredness. Easily provoked anger and irritation at annoying habits and quirks. There are little foxes destroying the crop of your marriage. Whatever they are, you need to catch them! Isn't it funny how the same things that attracted us to our husbands in the first place can be the very things we later try to change?

If we keep reading in the Song of Solomon, it isn't too long after the beautiful feast in the bridal chambers that the Shulamite maiden lets the little foxes intrude. Solomon comes to her chambers for some (more) loving! She provides a variety of excuses. This is my paraphrase. "I am already in bed and my robe is off. Do I really have to get up and put it on again? And I've just taken a bath. My feet are clean...if I get up and let you in, they'll get all dirty again" (Song of Solomon 5:2-3).

I'm betting Solomon thought the fact she was ready for bed was perfect timing! But by the time she rethinks all of this and gets up to go after him, he is already gone. Sulking, perhaps. Feeling rejected.

What she had once welcomed with beautiful and racy poetry, she now found an irritating intrusion. Isn't it something how quickly we decide that we don't really want to please our mate if it means any inconvenience to ourselves? We convince ourselves that our spouses are unreasonable. Demanding, even.

Writer Cyndy Salzmann shares a classic example. "You see, the best thing I ever did for my marriage was to quit spitting into my husband's sink." She describes how she was using *his* side of the double, master bath sinks in their new home for brushing her teeth. She would then move to her side for hair and makeup. After a few weeks, her husband realized this wasn't an oversight and politely requested that she use her own sink.

Cyndy reports laughing hysterically. "You have to be kidding!... I'm the mother of your children: I should be able to spit anywhere I want!"[9]

She rationalized that since she was the sink cleaner, it was okay. Then she changed her plan to "sink subterfuge" (spitting when he wasn't around) and continued for more than a year. Gradually she allowed God to convict her that she needed to honor her husband, even in this small matter.

Greg and I have had issues of our own in this arena. Three years ago, just months after we had finally finished remodeling our 98-year-old dream/nightmare farmhouse, we lost it in a tornado. In the following few weeks, I was a tornado of activity myself—trying to find a new house for us, grieving, moping, and then busily using allocated insurance funds to purchase our needs and create a home as fast as possible.

I had asked Greg to come with me on several occasions to buy furniture or pick out paint, but the answer was always, "That's okay, honey. Go ahead. I'm swamped with stuff of my own to take care of."

I was a woman on a mission; a bit too late I discovered it was the wrong one. With great care I chose a traditional "daddy" chair for Greg. However, I placed it at an angle in a corner and then set an iron basket lamp behind it. Furthermore, I had forgotten to get an ottoman for Greg's feet to rest on and there was no little table nearby for him to place his drinks or remote. Still, I thought it looked really cute in that location.

Greg did not.

He could not see the television from that angle. He had to reach way down to the floor to rescue his tea from the girls' running feet. Bottom line: He felt unable to relax.

The next year, I made a halfhearted attempt to rearrange the furniture, but any new placement of the daddy chair didn't do the room justice. Grudgingly, I moved the basket lamp and put the chair flush with the wall. Then I decided to leave well enough alone. Meanwhile, Greg moved across the room to sit on the loveseat. He could see the TV, but this seemingly small issue festered.

This year, we have done some really hard work on our marriage. Because of what we thought was a temporary but necessary state of schedules and circumstances, we had allowed our marriage to assume "roommate" status. Oh, we had the added bonus of permission to sleep together, but our emotional intimacy had deteriorated at an alarming rate. More than we had known.

Among the issues that were dug up and worked through was the saga of the daddy chair. During the same time of the family room fiasco, I had marched over Greg's feelings by fixing our bedroom while he was out of town and painted a bathroom sloppily—one of the seven deadly sins in his book—after he asked me to wait until he got back. Waiting in the midst of a mess makes me crazy, so instead of verbalizing that and seeking a compromise, I plowed ahead.

Furthermore, thinking his anger was of the teasing sort, I had glossed over it, laughed about it, and never apologized. I had spent an inordinate number of months in quiet, righteous indignation, certain that the growing emotional distance between us was entirely his fault. When he brought this to my attention, to say that I was defensive would be like saying that Shaquille O'Neal is tall and plays basketball fairly well.

God literally woke me up nights, working on *my* heart until I scraped scabs from it and allowed my husband to share *his* heart with me. "You know, Cinso," my husband began. "It's not really about the chair at all. It's about your attitude. Instead of following my leadership and listening to my requests, you ignored me, and that hurt me. In every other home we've had, you've solicited my input. When it was important to me, you listened. When it wasn't a big deal, I let you do whatever you wanted because you're better at this stuff than me. But you have *always,* until this house, created a place of honor. A place that was all mine. A spot you knew I'd enjoy, one that everyone could tell belonged to me."

The heart of the matter was as simple as it was complex: I had failed to give my hardworking husband honor because of my blind selfishness. It cost us. It costs me still to even write such a sentence.

The loveseat isn't in our family room anymore—I sold it while Greg was at work one day. When he came home that evening, it was obvious where his place was. He thrives there, working from his laptop, putting down his Pepsi, clanking the remotes together, reigning as he should as the head of our home. It is a powerful symbol and a reminder to me.

An unknown writer observed, "A man holds such a tender place in his wife's heart when the marriage begins, but soon seems just a whisper above a stray animal." Those words pierced my heart.

What about you, precious friend? Is your heart still honeymoon tender toward your husband? Do you cheerfully yield to his requests, even if they seem as silly as spitting in your own sink or moving his furniture? Do you really want to recapture your marriage or are you stubbornly digging your heels in, waiting for him to go first? "He who finds a wife finds what is good..." (Proverbs 18:22). May it be true of all of us who are blessed enough to have the title, wife.

> *"A successful marriage requires falling in love many times, always with the same person."*
>
> MIGNON MCLAUGHLIN

For something that so many novels, movies, and greeting cards are written about, this love thing can be pretty darn hard to nail down, can't it? Just the other night we watched a Charlie Brown Valentine special. There were several laugh-out-loud moments. Even the cartoon females had their men trapped in a dilemma of trying to do or say the right thing to please their best girl. Little Sally, ever hopeful, stood openhanded in front of her self-proclaimed "Sweet Baboo" Linus with great expectations that were not met.

Meanwhile, an ever dedicated Snoopy typed Valentine verse after verse for Lucy's approval. (You know what happens next!) Lucy reads the first one and the next and the next and huffs dismissively before stating that women want romance every minute of every day and these offerings are insufficient.

It's pretty sad when we begin to identify with the quest for love as defined by the Peanuts gang, isn't it? And yet we *do* identify. We throw out lofty ideas and petulant requests, only to fling a figurative typewriter page back in our spouse's face, stomping our feet and saying, if not in words, then with our displeasure: "That's not what I wanted! Don't you get it?"

It seems as if we're not always sure what we want. Perhaps Charlie Brown summed it up best: "Love makes you do strange things." I pray that these next chapters will give some shape and focus to our nameless desires and restless yearnings.

I recently looked over some notes I had written when Greg and I were asked to share at a church Valentine banquet, just three years after we were married.

> Greg is patient, kind, intelligent, funny, witty, generally unselfish, tender, hard-headed, nearly as stubborn as I am, and therefore, is up to the task of keeping me in line! He even has his romantic moments!
>
> He has admirably tackled the task of godly fatherhood, as I've presented him with three children in three years of marriage! This one is due to arrive two weeks before our third anniversary. Bachelorhood broad-sided! Yet he is still smiling!
>
> I feel blessed, because this is not only the man who can make my knees go weak with a look or a touch, the man who will run with me through our youth, but he is also the man I want to grow old with. To sit on porch swings with and rock our babies and then to sit again much later with our grandchildren, swinging more slowly and reminiscing.

Now before you want to get up and find an airline vomit bag, let me just say that while those words are still very true, my *feelings* have not always matched the words I wrote a decade ago.

My husband and I have a huge enlargement of our favorite wedding picture. Our smiles are glowing. Greg is unbearably handsome in his formal tuxedo. I am willowy and beaming in my flowing dress, carrying red tulips, shoes daintily buckled with pearl buttons. He is in the process of twirling me around. Snap! The photographer froze that moment in time forever.

You have photographs of your own big moments. We all need to make sure that when our wedding photographers captured bliss, they didn't merely embalm the moment. We need to actively resurrect these moments again and again throughout our married life.

In writing this book, I have had much reason to ponder and research why that is. Where do they go and why do they need to be recaptured? From the survey responses, emails, articles, books, and interviews conducted, I know that this nebulous, waffling ebb and surge of feelings is often true, at least in seasons, of every single marriage in existence.

This is a book about learning the practical tools of relationships so that we will learn with our head what ought to exist in our heart; it's a book about working at our marriages, but not so much that we forget to have fun and breathe creativity, kindness, generosity, and adventure into them. By doing this, we will experience the joy of committed love, of knowing that sweet times are often just over the hedge of dark ones. That God blesses a vow kept, a promise honored.

CHOCOLATE-COVERED QUESTIONS

1. Do you think fairy tales and Hollywood screen versions of marriages have affected our expectations of what marriage should look like? What is the best thing about marriage in your opinion? The most difficult?

2. Is our marriage what you expected it to be? Why or why not?

3. Do you agree or disagree that sometimes things are better left unsaid in a marriage? If you agree, what kinds of things?

4. What about marriage surprised you most?

5. Do you, or did you, hide things from each other in order to present yourself in the best light?

SCRIPTURE

*"There is no fear in love. But perfect love
drives out fear" (1 John 4:18).*

HOT CHOCOLATE TOPIC

What fears did you have, if any, about our
marriage as our wedding drew closer?

GOODNIGHT KISS

*Honey, if I had the choice of whether or not to
do it all over again, I'd still say "Yes!"*

WHAT IS THE RIGHT AGE TO GET MARRIED?

*Twenty-three is the best age because you
know the person FOREVER by then.*

CAMILLE, AGE 10

What Lies Beneath
Expectations and Reality

*He seldom carries forward from the ledger
of today into tomorrow's account.*

LORD CHANDOS ON WINSTON CHURCHILL'S
FORGIVING NATURE

O ur wedding was beautiful. It went off without a single hitch. Red tulip bouquets. Wearing red dresses, my mother and my little sister stood guard. I had found the perfect dress and a comb with tulips wound through my hair.

My daddy and my four-and-a-half-year-old daughter walked me down the aisle to the wedding processional from *The Sound of Music*. The church was packed with students, family, and friends. I managed to sing "When I Fall in Love" to Greg without crying. The music, candles, vows, reception, and cake were wonderful. We ran through a cloud of bubbles to the waiting limousine. We were whisked away to Tulsa where we were to spend our first night as husband and wife before flying out to Cancun the next morning. When Greg signed us in as "Mr. and Mrs. Greg Dagnan," I literally felt faint with joy.

A grinning bellboy put our luggage on a cart and stopped the elevator outside the honeymoon suite. He unlocked our door with a flourish. We were unprepared for the incredible sight that greeted us.

A rather large maid sat on the edge of a king-size bed, smoking, eating potato chips, and watching television. She turned to the bell-hop with annoyance. "What you doin' bringin' dese people in heah? You know dis is my hangout when the air conditionin' is broken in the downstairs! Huh? Dis is my hangout!"

The bellboy hustled us out and back down to the registration desk. The hotel manager was extremely apologetic when he heard what had happened. My husband stated some rather obvious facts. "This is *not* the reception I had planned for my bride on our first night together. I booked the *nonsmoking* honeymoon suite, and I'd really planned for the two of us to be the only ones in the room!"

Meanwhile, I had recovered from the shock and started to snicker. It really was comical, if not very romantic. They moved us to a different suite, albeit not the honeymoon suite, and threw in roses, chilled champagne, complimentary dinners for two, and a coupon for a free stay the next year.

Doubtless, we all have our honeymoon tales and they're all probably different. However, when it comes to digging beneath the beauty of a ceremony and the relaxation of a honeymoon, we probably all share a set of common concerns and fears when it comes to our marriages.

Seasons of a Marriage

My husband and I team teach a Sunday school class to couples ranging in age from 24 to 55. About every year and a half we do a "marriage intensive" for several weeks. It remains a big draw. What always astonishes us is that no matter how short or how long the duration of the marriage, couples continue to tell us how much they need relationship reminders. We share many of the same general worries.

A few years ago, we asked the class to write down their top concerns or fears about their marital relationships. If you look over this list, you'll probably see your own concerns represented.

- ♥ Lack of intimacy causing roving eyes
- ♥ He/she might no longer find me attractive

♥ He/she might lose interest in me

♥ Keeping connected with our busy lives

♥ Neglecting our relationship and/or having an empty marriage

♥ Balancing time with children and time with spouse (Yep, all the women listed children first.)

♥ How we will relate to each other after the kids are grown up

♥ My spouse having an affair or leaving me because I fail to live up to expectations

♥ Knowing that someday one of us will likely end up alone due to old age/death

♥ Not being able to provide for my wife and family (This particular concern was listed on nearly every male response sheet—take note of this insight into your husband.)

♥ Not following God's plan or knowing God's will for our marriage

Overall, the biggest wants and hopes expressed were: "I want to know how to be the best spouse possible" and "I need some ideas on how to rekindle passion and romance."

Chances are that you'll encounter one or more of these concerns at various points in your marriage. Author and counselor Gary Chapman calls these points "seasons" and observes that there are four distinct seasons in marriage, each with their own attitudes, actions, and emotions.

> Winter is a negative season characterized by hurt, anger, and disappointment. In winter, we tend to think the worst of our spouse, avoiding them or withdrawing deep into ourselves. The verbal continuum may run the spectrum from noisy arguments to lethal silence.

> The spring season in marriage is hopeful, positive, and active. Just like the same season in nature, brand new green growth and the signs of wonderful change are everywhere.

Couples may feel buoyant and ebullient. They're willing to tackle issues with gusto, think the best of their spouse, and energetically invest in the relationship.

Summer is a happily settled feeling with happiness and satisfaction pervading. Couples see that their marriage is beautiful, but without resentment recognize that the relationship needs work and water, just as our plants and summer gardens do. Summer marriage seasons involve comfortable companionship, travel (at least to mental destinations), and activity.

Fall sets in with sadness and apprehension; that nagging feeling that something doesn't seem quite right in the relationship. One or both of you may be thinking, "Something has to change," even if you can't quite pinpoint what you want that change to be.

Concern and uncertainty tag along during the day and if not addressed and corrected, the marriage can be neglected or viewed with apathy. I call this putting the marriage on autopilot. It's dangerous, because a discontented restlessness can occur, making this a prime season for affairs.[1]

Marital seasons can progress in a cyclical fashion, go back and forth, or tumble over each other. Seasons can occur or change based on events which happen within or to the marriage (birth, death, move, promotion, depression, unfaithfulness, a marriage seminar, conference, or retreat). You can move through several seasons in the space of a few months, or they may be present during different, longer "eras" or stages of your marriage.

If you're stuck in a season that you don't like, it won't likely change unless someone is willing to break the cycle. And here's another yucky truth, girlfriends—that someone may have to be you. I won't lie to you—it's so hard to be the big person and go first. Apologize first. Work on your own character first. Be a student of your husband all over again. Become a prayer warrior. Stop waiting for him to change first. Let's spend the next few chapters together, studying how that can be done.

～

"Honey," Eve called to Adam. "Do you like the large fig leaf best? Or do you think I'd look better stringing a batch of those gorgeous colored autumn leaves together?"

"Look," Adam replied in a bored tone, "it doesn't make any difference to me. I think you look great in anything. Personally, I like you best au naturel, the way you looked when I first saw you."

Eve huffed off and went in search of other options and a debate about whether gardenias or roses looked best in her hair. As Richard Armour humorously observed, "Until Eve arrived, this was a man's world."

Yep, it's an age-old conflict. As the saying goes, "When women are depressed, they either eat or go shopping. When men are depressed they invade another country. It's a whole different way of thinking."

The wonderful news about blending these differences is the potential to generate pure bliss. The downside is, approximately 37 hours after the honeymoon, we realize it takes hard work. Neither person's expectations are necessarily wrong, they're just different.

> *"The most impressive example of tolerance is*
> *a golden wedding anniversary."*
> ANONYMOUS

Great Expectations

When we remodeled our old farmhouse, all of us lived in the same room for five and a half long months. We'd lie awake at night and listen to the mice eat our belongings. Tears and trauma notwithstanding, it was still an adventure to us—choosing things for each room, planning the decorating, hanging at Lowe's, and haunting antique shops.

The experience of shaping and restoring our home was a lot like that of marriage. While the adventure was new, it was sparkling. "Fresh smells, fun surprises, and new discoveries make each day snap, crackle and pop. Sure, there's work to be done, but the newness takes away the hassle. As time passes, however, things change. Slowly, almost imperceptibly, the grit of responsibility mixed with the grind of routine starts to take its toll."[2]

Whether you begin life in a new house or a tiny apartment, decorating in a curious style called "Early Sigler Basement" (fill in your maiden name!) is still loads of fun. At first. Unwrapping all those beautifully wrapped gifts from the endless wedding registries you filled out. Carefully choosing a place for the furniture you do have. Budgeting is even fun before you discover that finances can turn into a Shakespearean tragedy if there is no wise counsel applied. Let's face it. To quote my girls, doing stuff when it's new is just "funner."

The marriage you want—a good one—takes a lot of time. Author and marriage counselor Kevin Leman states that from his experience, "it takes most couples at least ten years to break out of their families of origin and start building a new one."[3] That translates into a lot of adjustments, some remodeling of the soul, and a release of some unrealistic, if romantic, expectations. For most every woman I speak with, that means letting go of the much-craved, but highly unlikely, possibility that your husband can read your mind. I know, I know...all of us long for our dream man to recognize when we're down and need cheering up, to notice that the house is a complete wreck and pitch in unasked, to come home and whisk us away for a dinner out, a weekend retreat, or an evening in Paris.

Our fantasies, at least mine anyway, border on the ludicrous. I constantly need to realistically evaluate the current circumstances of our marriage. We have four young girls, two ancient cars, and one income; many of my hidden expectations simply aren't possible just now. Let's lead the way by giving our husbands a teensy break.

In his book *Love of a Lifetime*, Dr. James Dobson states, "[Your husband] is no more equipped to resolve your entire package of emotional needs than you are to become his sexual dream machine every twenty-four hours. Both partners have to settle for human foibles and faults and irritability and fatigue and occasional night-time 'headaches.' A good marriage is not one where perfection reigns: It is a relationship where a healthy perspective overlooks a multitude of 'unresolvables.'"[4] And there will be plenty of those!

If we are honest, we will admit to taking a problem in one facet of our marriages and, depending on the time of month, time of day, how much month is left at the end of the money, or how much sleep we've gotten or haven't, extrapolate this problem into every area of our lives. We give something that is quite small a huge area of influence, and this makes us and our husbands miserable. We need to stop.

My husband neatly summed up this tendency by borrowing a line from the once ubiquitous *NYPD Blue:* "High maintenance, like a broad." Much as I'd like to, I just can't argue with that most of the time.

Once you're married, the potential for irritation increases a hundredfold. No longer can you say good-bye at the end of a romantic evening and retreat to the shelter of your dorm room or your own apartment. The time of waiting and longing is over. Remember thinking, "Won't it be great when we're finally married? You won't have to leave at all! We can spend as long as we want talking and then curl up and sleep together!" Sigh.

And much about it *is* wonderful and romantic. You have permission to stay all night together, to experience the pleasures of physical love in a guilt-free setting, to work on your household together. But this togetherness is also the source of much conflict.

When Greg and I were first married, I had no idea how strongly the images of my parents' marriage and their role divisions had affected me. I knew exactly what the "boy" jobs around the house were and what the "girl" responsibilities were as well.

Boy Chores
- ♥ Take out the trash
- ♥ Mow the lawn and maintain outside house repairs

- ♥ Take care of all car maintenance
- ♥ Be in charge of all outdoor grilling
- ♥ Pull the trash to the curb on trash day
- ♥ Scrape windshields and shovel walks
- ♥ Entertain the children
- ♥ Be the "heavy" when Mom needs back up

Girl Chores

- ♥ Buy groceries
- ♥ Plan and prepare most meals
- ♥ Care for children
- ♥ Deal with potty training
- ♥ Dust and vacuum house weekly
- ♥ Decorate and maintain the inside of the house
- ♥ Do dishes, laundry, and ironing

Greg, on the other hand, had very different ideas. Greg was the only child of later-in-life parents. They doted on him, not so much with physical affection, but with dedicated service. His dad faithfully went with him to all scouting events. His mother prepared him a different meal if he didn't like what they were having. She even made his bed through high school!

When we returned from our honeymoon, I fully expected that our home life together would fall neatly along those lines without any discussion. Trash pick up day came and I waited for Greg to notice the trash cans were full. I waited for him to empty them into the garbage bin in the garage and haul them to the curb. And I waited, and waited, and waited some more. We both have a wide stubborn streak so I let the trash spill over, harboring a grudge and stomping around the house; he was blissfully unaware of the cause of my irritation. It was something that merited discussion, but it wasn't a full blown issue on the "Big Deal Scale" (we'll get to that in a second). We've even learned to laugh about it.

This can extend to other areas of married life as well. All of us have hidden expectations which we don't verbalize to our spouses. Dr. Leman calls these "rule books," and he estimates that those little suckers are behind 90 percent of all marital disagreements. For example, you may have a rule or expectation that your husband will always arrange for childcare when planning your dates. While he's at it, amaze you with the variety, creativity, and passion with which he plans said dates. (Stop laughing and work with me here!)

Now, if you never communicate this expectation and instead decide to pout silently as you wait for your monthly date to happen in this ideal fashion, you are only setting yourself up. When you do finally have a night out or a precious couple hours with your husband, you'll be fuming over something he knows nothing about—because you never *shared* your desires!

When we pull this refusal-to-communicate-because-if-you-loved-me-you-would-know-what-I-need, hop on our high horses, and ride them off into the sunset, we are miserably alone. Have you noticed this part? Crash! Expectations and reality collide.

Here's a moment of truth (and, I might add, truth hurts): One of the hardest things about marriage is making grown-up choices. Sometimes it's easier to live like we're still playing dress-up and make believe.

Grown-up choices are hard and marriage can make them harder. An interdependent relationship requires us to grow up quickly and learn lessons frequently. One of my favorite professors was my English composition teacher, Mrs. Jackina Stark. During my freshman year of college, she shared with us the story of her first year of young marriage. I think she was only 19 at the time of her nuptials. One night when her budget-conscious husband declined her request for take-out pizza, she was hurt and appalled. She ran upstairs to their bedroom, slammed the door, and poured out her hurt in her journal. She couldn't believe her husband could be cruel enough to deny her something as simple as pizza! *Not in the budget!* She fumed and didn't see how they could ever make it as a couple. She laughs now, 40 years later, but at the time it was a difficult choice for her to accept his fledgling leadership about their budget.

It doesn't necessarily get easier with time. A few days ago I could have taken an opportunity to do something I adore, singing and acting in our local Little Theatre. It would have cost me much time, much practice, and much sanity. I pled my case to Greg. He told me he would pray for me to have the sense to hear and heed God's will.

So, I took my case to God. The next morning the entry on my flip calendar for moms read: "Are you there for your family?" Grrr...this was going nowhere. I sought the godly counsel of people I respect. They agreed I could do this thing stunningly well, but didn't think it was wise with my current time commitments.

I can be pretty stubborn when I want something desperately, so I kept throwing out different fleeces which all came back as sopping wet sponges. At the very last minute I became resigned to submission. I hate to admit that it was reluctant submission, but it was. I listened to my husband's wise words, "We are building something, and I'm going to be upset if you mess it up, but not as upset as you will be with yourself."

I won't kid you, sacrifice is neither noble nor pleasant. Sometimes it's just hard.

Fault Patrol

Don't be on fault patrol. It seems that Satan's cleverness includes serving up our husband's faults on a continual basis after that first big disappointment. Despite the fact that this man never emitted a single bodily noise during courtship, when we get home from the honeymoon, we discover that he can belch the entire alphabet...and he thinks it's funny. We begin to notice that he chews his gum annoyingly. He often forgets to take out the trash. And why do his socks have to gather around, not in, the laundry basket in those wadded up, stupid little balls? Why can't he actually pull the socks out straight? Does he think I *like* to pick those dumb things up? You have the idea.

In fact, a horrible trait known as "Cross Complaining" is listed among Dr. Larry Halter's communication killers.[5] At its heart, cross complaining is an attempt to transfer the blame for a fault when your spouse brings up a criticism about you. When your mate comes to you with a genuine concern (complaint) you say, "Well, you've got a lot of nerve telling me that I don't spend enough time with you! You're the one who's always going to the stupid golf course or watching ESPN!" For the record, my husband notes that policemen won't take those types of complaints.

At that point the conversation spirals downward into a fault-finding session instead of a concerned reporting session. One of you claims the issue is "no big deal," while the other partner retreats, feeling invalidated. That's not a healthy thing to do because it isn't possible to tell someone how they *shouldn't* feel. It's one of the reasons that Greg and I have tried to live by this simple rule: If it is important to you, then it's important to me. In marriage we are to be one flesh. That means that if you hurt your husband, you are really hurting yourself too—of course this works in reverse also.

One man described his wife with these convicting statements: "She'd make an excellent district attorney! She has her process-servers out for any fault, and she keeps them working seven days a week, twenty-four hours a day!"[6] Ouch! Do you feel a twinge?

Other times, it's sheer stubbornness that keeps us from wanting to put our mate's needs above our own. Consider this often quoted story, reprinted in newspapers and magazines. I'm unsure of the original source, but each time I read it I crack up.

> A woman accompanied her husband to the doctor's office. After his checkup, the doctor called the wife into his office alone. He said, "Your husband is suffering from a very severe disease, combined with horrible stress. If you don't do the following, your husband will surely die: Each morning fix him a healthy breakfast. Be pleasant and make sure he is in a good mood. For lunch make him a nutritious meal. For dinner prepare an especially nice meal for him. Don't burden

him with chores, as he's probably had a hard day. Don't discuss your problems with him; it will only make his stress worse. And, most importantly, satisfy his every whim. If you can do this for the next ten months to a year, I think your husband will regain his health completely."

On the way home, the husband asked his wife, "What did the doctor say?"

"You're going to die," she replied.

The Big Deal Scale

One tool which has helped everyone in our family is something we call the "Big Deal Scale." Before (preferably) we blow up about something, we run it through this test.

- ♥ Is this problem, situation, request, or hurt going to matter to me tomorrow? Cola glass rings on the coffee table. Nah. Trying to "help" me by pressing the bake setting for dough rising in the bread machine? I'll pass on being upset unless we're expecting to bake homemade cinnamon rolls for Oprah, who's spending the night. And how likely is that, really?

- ♥ Will it still bother me next week? Toenail clippings, probably.

- ♥ Next month? Forgetting to tell me about an event until the day of? I can let it go.

- ♥ Next year? A habit of overwork? Yup. Better sit down and work out a compromise.

- ♥ Will it bug me in five years? Um...what were we fighting about? Keep mouth shut.

If the answer to the first two questions is no, you should probably let it go. Not everything is worthy of a federal case, complete with notes and prosecutorial ammunition. Not every issue is a fundamental one; choose your battles. You can only complain for so long until everything you say goes off the radar.

Ever notice that sometimes the fight between the two of you goes on so long that when someone eventually yells, "Truce!" you can no longer remember what the fight was about? See my point?

> *"Great events make me quiet and calm; it is only trifles that irritate my nerves."*
> QUEEN VICTORIA

In our marriage seminars, Greg always opens his section with this humorous list of classes covering some things he would like to teach me.

Silence, the Final Frontier: Where No Woman Has Gone Before

Communication 101: Tears, the Last Resort Not the First

Communication 201: Formulating a Thought Before Speaking

Telephone Skills: How to Hang the Phone Up

Do These Jeans Make Me Look Fat?: Why Men Lie

Combating the Imelda Marcos Syndrome: You Do Not Need 50 Pairs of Shoes

Classic Clothing: Wearing the Things You Already Have

The Undiscovered Side of Banking: Making Deposits

Greg then adds that I especially need that last one because if I can't make the checkbook balance, I believe we should just switch banks! "After I first presented her with this list," Greg relates, "I took a course myself that night, 'How to Make the Downstairs Couch More Comfortable for Sleeping'!"

He's joking of course, but he does have some wise insights for us girls. We tend to want to communicate everything about an event, including all of our feelings associated with any given happening. We tend to believe (or at least wish) that men will do the same when we ask questions. *Honey, how was your day? So, tell me all about your conference!*

"Wives," Greg says, "the best thing you can do when communicating with your husband is to let him get out the facts as they happened. Don't suspect him of hiding details if he shares everything in two minutes or less. He's not hiding anything; that's all he has to say!"

Humor Break

Rules Guys Wished Girls Knew

1. If you think you're fat, you probably are. Please don't ask us.

2. Anything you wear is fine. Really.

3. You can either ask us to do something OR tell us how you want it done—not both.

—selected from Children Change a Marriage
by Elisa Morgan and Carol Kuykendall

Family Boundaries

A few days ago I had the privilege of interviewing a wonderful trio of women, each of whom had celebrated their golden wedding anniversary and even decades beyond! I curled up in a back pew of our church's sanctuary, my pen flying over my lined notepad. Before my eyes, I saw these distinguished, impeccably dressed ladies with twinkles in their smiles transform into the young brides they once were. An instant bond formed as I asked questions and took in their answers.

It quickly became apparent that things in the 1940s weren't all that different from what they are today. A couple of the women mentioned possessive or critical in-laws as one of the biggest obstacles in their early marriage. One woman lamented about her visits to the in-laws. "We went out to that farm so many times, it's a wonder we didn't get a divorce!" She turned eyes like blue saucers my way, "Don't put that in the book!" She smiled broadly. "Just tell them that you have troubles along the way, but you have to get over 'em!" Her partner in crime reminisced, "Young people complain too much about things these days. It's better to accept a few things that aren't going to change and just get over them!"

It's hard to be offended by any of their candid, forceful advice because they've clearly lived through the good and the bad and have triumphed. Their memories were sprinkled with hilarity, poignancy, and extravagant praise of their husbands. They nodded in camaraderie of understanding when I told them about some of the similar obstacles couples face today.

Tim's mom called him and his new bride, Kelly, every night at dinner time for three years. She inquired about their plans, asked their menu, and wondered whether or not her son was getting proper nutrition and being served his favorite foods. Tim didn't want to offend his mother, so he put off any confrontation and encouraged Kelly to be patient for just a while longer.

Sherry's parents routinely called on Sunday mornings to make sure the couple was attending church. If they answered the phone in the morning, they were scolded for not getting up in time for church. If they chose to ignore the phone or were indeed at morning services, they were given a pop quiz about the name of the church, the sermon topic, and whether or not they'd placed membership anywhere. Sherry and Ted grew to dread Sundays and the weekly "church check" call.

Among the potential conflicts in any marriage, there are parents with good intentions and grown up children who want to honor them. Sooner or later we must face the fact that we didn't just marry our spouse, we also married his family, his upbringing, and his expectations. When that is finally understood, we can survey the territory, put down our own firm "couple roots," and stake our claims.

And just to add a new twist, we face the scourge of technology. Cell phones are becoming the second umbilical cord. It's nearly impossible to get away from anyone without deliberate, conscientious action anymore! If you hear ringing in your ears too often and during inopportune moments, explain to both sets of parents that there will be certain times you won't be answering your phone. If parents live out of town, schedule a weekly time to call so they will have something to look forward to. Mail them some of the kids' school work or home videos and plan visits with anticipation. A sense of loss is often the root of the problem; the development of connectivity is nearly always part of the solution.

It's vital for spouses to stand up for each other in the face of family conflict, to initiate a healthy separation from extended familial ties, and to gently encourage balance between work obligations and family fun. Discuss appropriate and reasonable boundaries with each other and then work on a plan for implementation. It's best to have each of you speak to your own parents, presenting a firm, united, but tactful, front.

For example, if your mother feels that you must spend Easter, Christmas, Independence Day, and Thanksgiving with her and only wants to share you with the in-laws on Arbor Day, Labor Day, and President's Day, you may have to work out a rotating schedule with plenty of advance notice.

If you live close enough, perhaps you can spend Christmas Eve with one family and Christmas Day with the other. Or, as one family did after years of feeling like the holiday season was frantic, not festive, you could announce that you are staying home and parents are welcome to visit you!

Begin new traditions as a couple and be willing to change them as children (or more children) come along. Your creativity and hospitality might open up a whole new way of thinking and relating for your extended families. You might plan for an annual Labor Day picnic with both sides of the family, a summer family reunion, or a Christmas brunch hosted at your home or at a different home each year. Breathing new life into your family's traditions will do the same for others. Okay, maybe they won't all want to face change, but the life cycle includes honoring some long time traditions and also embracing new ones.

God commands that no matter the season of our marriages, our spouse needs to be our first earthly priority. Too much is riding on our marriage for him *not* to be first. When the expectations do crumble or you are rounding up a master list of his faults, remember that he is your home, your today, your future, and your family.

CHOCOLATE-COVERED QUESTIONS

1. What was the hardest adjustment for you in our marriage?

2. What is it like being married to me?

3. Are there family boundaries that we still need to put in place?

4. What is one expectation you had for our marriage that has been fulfilled? What is one that was totally unrealistic?

5. How does the Big Deal Scale change your perspective on a recent argument? How will this help your perspective?

SCRIPTURE

"If a man has recently married, he must not be sent to war or have any other duty laid on him. For one year he is to be free to stay at home and bring happiness to the wife he has married" (Deuteronomy 24:5).

HOT CHOCOLATE TOPIC

On a sliding scale of 1-10, with 10 being the best, how do you rate our marriage overall? If this score is lower than you're satisfied with, what would be your suggestions of the top three ways we could make it better?

GOODNIGHT KISS

I've liked almost everything I've dug up from beneath so far!

"Chocolate is known to be good for the heart, and for mood boosting, but researchers have recently identified a component in cocoa that reduces platelet clumping, helping blood flow smoothly!"

—*TIME*, DECEMBER 4, 2006

The Sweetness of Covenant
Forgiveness and Promises

Grow old along with me. The best is yet to be;
The last of life, for which the first was made.

ROBERT BROWNING

As women, we probably already know that it's wise for us to chart our monthly cycles. When PMS (I've heard it dubbed "Princess Must Scream") strikes, most of us are moodier, have our feelings hurt more easily, and may be a bit snippier with our mates. One couple made a "hold harmless" clause for cranky exchanges during that week.

But it is also true that men have moods, almost chartable times when they are down in the dumps. Charlie Shedd gave his engaged daughter Karen some excellent words of wisdom.

> Try your best not to go down into the swamps of despair when he goes down...It is so easy for you to become melancholy when he becomes melancholy.
>
> Because you love him so much...it may appear on the surface that you could help him best by glumming it through together! (But) if you can keep your heart filled with high-level kindness when he is down, you will really contribute more to his recovery than by almost any other method.[1]

John Gray explains that when they are confronted with a problem or a bad mood, men withdraw and literally morph into cave men. We need to recognize that this need is as legitimate as others. Men tend to resolve issues best alone; we women want to commiserate and talk it out with others. Like so many potentially divisive issues, we do ourselves a favor when we recognize that this is not bad, just *different*.

"The world is unnerved by a truly masculine man, and so it tries to socialize men *away* from all that is fierce and wild and passionate. Yet God made men the way they are because we *need* them to be the way they are. As Christina Hoff Sommers said, 'The energy, competitiveness, and corporeal daring of normal, decent males are responsible for much of what is right in the world.'"[2] I read that and thought that to completely change my husband would be to erase much of what made me fall for him in the first place.

I adore the fact that when I lie down on his chest, and he holds me in his arms at night, his chest is hard and his arms are sculpted. My softness complements this and the contrast is delightful. I *like* it that he gets up to investigate all strange noises and is my mouse trapper and spider killer extraordinaire. He finds my lost things, centers me when my world is spinning, and supports my endeavors—even the crazy ones. He is a moral man of integrity; he is my true north. And I'll let you in on a secret: Sometimes his way of seeing things is better than mine.

When we demand our own way or that our spouse copes with a problem in our way (the right way!), we are driving wedges into our union. In his book *The 10 Commandments of Marriage*, Ed Young lists the first amusing commandment as "Thou Shalt Not Be a Selfish Pig!"[3] Do I hear any oinking?

Feelings, Something More Than Feelings

There is perhaps no other area where women feel more misunderstood than this one. Feelings are what cause us to want to run back home at the first sign of disharmony. I love Dr. Kevin Leman's list about facts on feelings. Here they are, along with my comments.

1. **Your feelings aren't right or wrong.** They just are. Whew, that's a relief!

2. **You have a right to express them.** Just don't take that as a license to vent without self-control.

3. **You don't always have to act on them.** This is the toughest feeling fact for me. I have similar trouble distinguishing between wants and needs. After all, I wouldn't want it if I didn't need it! I'm not advocating that you never act on a feeling, but our feelings are so transient that if we kept a journal of them, we might list twelve different ones in a fifteen minute period. Depending on the situation, consider waiting a day, praying about it, or at least counting to ten.

4. **You should never ask your mate, "Why do you feel that way?" (That places the emphasis on the cause and not the feeling.)** A close cousin to that is, "You shouldn't feel like that." We tend to invalidate feelings, causing our partner to become defensive.

5. **Feelings draw you closer to your mate, but judgments push you apart.** [4] Just because your husband has a different opinion or different interests than you do does not place him in the wrong.

True Forgiveness

After reading more than 80 books, taking 100 surveys, conducting interviews, and listening to men and women across the country talk about marriage and relationships, I'd go so far as to say that I believe selfishness is the root of all marital problems. That means saying the words "I'm sorry" and "I forgive you" must be integral to a healthy relationship. Forgiveness does not excuse bad behavior. It doesn't say everything that happened was okay. It does, however, lead to our spiritual health. Jesus says that God will deal with us harshly unless we forgive our brother from the heart (Matthew 18:35).

Forgiveness also means something else—we don't continually throw the offense back in our spouse's face during future arguments. Once something is forgiven, although we will likely still remember, we need to leave it buried. Sniffing around the backyard of past hurts in order to dig up a wrong is like leaving a corpse on display. Yuck! Unforgiveness pervades our spirits and erects a barrier between us and God. "Holding a grudge is like drinking poison and waiting for the other person to keel over," said a wise sage.

When I was in the fourth or fifth grade, I had a terrible time learning my multiplication tables. Every night after supper, I sat at the table with a yellow legal pad and copied the times tables. I couldn't play or do anything fun until I had finished. It was tedious. One Sunday evening my daddy preached a sermon on Peter's infamous question about forgiveness, "How many times do I have to do it?" Jesus answered, "Seventy-seven times" (Matthew 18:21-22). I threw up my hands and said, "That's 490!" I'm sure that my parents didn't intend for me to learn that lesson so I could make tally marks when someone wronged me, but that's exactly what I did in the post-honeymoon years. Somewhere around year four, I began to keep a score pad in my head of all the wrongs, real and imagined, which Greg had committed against me. I tallied them up, and when I felt he was coming dangerously close to the cut off, I threw up walls. Instead of erasing those marks with grace, I let them become etched on my heart. My behavior was a great deal like The Fonz on *Happy Days*. When it was my turn to confess my wrongdoing, it wouldn't come out! "I'm szzzz...szzzz..." I just couldn't complete the apology.

Relearning the Art of Listening

Remember those early days of courtship? Oh, the time we spent primping, trying to look so good that it seemed only casual effort had been required. We changed outfits, game to go wherever with our beloved. We spent hours talking—it seemed that we would never run out of things to say. Undivided attention to our sweetheart was natural.

Such events were still common in the early days of our marriage, but then life intruded. Our husbands tried telling us about their days, their goals, their feelings, their desires, but we didn't receive their tales with the same enthusiasm. Sometimes we interrupted them with a list of those past transgressions we were supposed to forgive and leave behind. Sometimes we rolled our eyes, sighed under our breath, interrupted or attempted to continue reading or doing the dishes while they talked.

One day, they stopped.

What happened? Remember, for our men to unburden themselves, they need to feel safe and accepted. To really listen to someone is to affirm their worth. When we stop and "listen with our eyes," as two-year-old Emmy beseeched me to do one day, we tell our husbands that nothing we are doing is more important.

Perhaps it's time for a quick refresher course on listening, or at least listening correctly.

Free exchanges thrive in an atmosphere of trust.

There are three Cs that need to be put on the trash pile in order for trust to flourish: Contempt, Complaining, Curtailing.

One of the biggest threats to communication is treating the speaker with disrespect. Dr. Emerson Eggerichs has done some excellent research uncovering the deepest basic needs of males and females. Not surprisingly, for the man it is respect; for the woman it is love. If these are not met, something he calls the "Crazy Cycle" results. Without love, she doesn't show him respect, so he doesn't show her love. In order to break it, something has to change. Contempt is the opposite of respect. Eggerichs mentions that a simple application of the admonition to respectful behavior in 1 Peter 3:2 is that a wife is "to display a respectful facial expression and tone when he fails to be the man she wants."[5] Catherine the Great phrased it this way, "Praise loudly, blame softly."

Seems simple. Makes sense. So why don't we give this sort of unconditional respect even when we know God asks us to? Because, as my high school students were always telling me, respect has to be earned. Well, doesn't it? Yes, but there is another type of respect that is different. For example, we are to respect our elders and treat them deferentially simply because of their status. We treat our bosses at work with respect because of their position of authority. It should be the same with our husbands. They are in a God given position of authority, and God says, "Show proper respect to everyone" (1 Peter 2:17). Notice it doesn't say anything about showing respect to only those who earn it.

Being respectful doesn't mean that we must agree with every decision, nor does it mean that we cannot offer suggestions of our own; however, it does mean that the manner in which we disagree conveys respect. It also means that we must *decide* to believe that our spouse does not *intend* disrespect. Greg and I call this giving each other the benefit of the doubt.

Complaining is a side effect of disrespect. We hover, looking for things that are being done wrong, that are overlooked, and that aren't as we expected. Dr. Eggerichs asks, "Why do some women feel so free to make comments like, 'You're not the man I thought you were' to their husbands and expect them to remain unaffected?"[6] As a general rule, men are taller, stronger, and bigger than women, so we have mistakenly viewed that as a sign that they don't really have feelings (except, perhaps in wailing country love songs). Our chronic complaining carves deep hurts in a relationship. I am so guilty of this because I find it easy to rationalize my complaining as "venting my feelings" or "giving voice to my unhappiness."

But to continue this cycle is to destroy the very interactions we are so desperately craving. "When the wife flatly says her husband will have to earn her respect before she gives him any, she leaves the husband in a lose-lose situation. Now he's responsible for both love and respect in the relationship. He must unconditionally love his wife and he also must earn her respect. Is it any wonder he shuts down in the face of all that?"[7]

Curtailing is what I call jump-rope conversation. In this situation I am not truly listening to Greg, I am formulating my rebuttal to what he is saying and waiting for a break in the conversation so that I can jump in with my point of view. Are anyone else's toes bleeding?

Our messages must match our tones and our actions.

I am sure this scenario never happens in your home, but it has happened in ours. Greg comes home from work, and he has innocently forgotten some little something that was vitally important to me. He walks into the kitchen where I have started supper and attempts to embrace me. Swatting him away, I give him a cursory greeting and continue with loud chopping and stirring.

"Honey? Is something wrong?"

I bite my tongue to keep from saying something smart like, "Ya think?" Instead, I reply, "Nothing's wrong (cabinet door slam) and no, I don't want to talk about it!" Hear that mixed message? I am a cabinet slammer in search of a mind reader!

Remember that communication is 58 percent nonverbal (that's way bad for us cabinet slammers), 35 percent tone of voice (frankly I can score pretty low on that one too), and only 7 percent your actual words.

How much better to give a warm and genuine welcome (aided by much prayer and power of the Holy Spirit) and then to say, "Greg, it really hurt my feelings that you didn't..." and fill in the blank with a concrete example of whatever it is.

Try to avoid the backdoor barge in too. If the Marines offered a specialty in this type of messaging, I would receive top honors. For example, instead of plainly asking Greg to clean the bathroom (one of his agreed upon jobs in our division of labor) when I am fed up, I might say snidely, "I can totally see why you haven't found time to clean the bathrooms yet. You've been so very busy watching TV." That's wrong. I *should* say, "Honey, I'm glad you've gotten the chance to relax after your hard week. I would really appreciate it if you'd clean the bathroom now."

Mirror, mirror on the couch.

As a detective and SWAT team negotiator, my husband is a

student of something called *kinesics,* or the study of non-verbal behavior. Closed postures include closed legs and closed arms. The higher and tighter the cross, the more defensive the person is. Leaning forward, palms up, and eye contact (which must break every seven seconds, or it's considered staring) are all signs of openness, of receptivity. Refusing to make eye contact is a sign of disengaging. Greg studies this body language to obtain confessions and solve crimes, but it will also come in handy as we seek to improve the atmosphere of our homes.

Try mirroring your husband's posture, making eye contact, and allowing sufficient time for reflection so you can process what he is saying. Hold his words back up to him. "I want to make sure that I understood you correctly. Are you saying that you think going to Branson this weekend isn't a good idea?"

Don't toss around ugly phrases like smoke bombs. "You always" or "You never" probably shouldn't be voiced. It only *feels* like always or never. Instead, say, "Whenever this happens *I* feel like you don't care about me."

Gary Smalley teaches a very effective technique for getting your spouse to understand your feelings. It's called painting a word picture. After a marriage seminar, Greg and I decided to give it a try. Greg and I had placed a small wager with each other, one that I had won. The prize I chose was for him to take an entire day off work and spend it with me, focused on us.

Around lunch time he got a call from the station. They really wanted to consult with him about a case, but they weren't ordering him in. The case seemed fascinating, so suffused with excitement, Greg decided to go in. I was hurt, mad, and disillusioned. I decided to paint him a picture. I told him, "I feel like I'm about seven years old. You've been promising to take me to this fabulous amusement park and go with me on my favorite ride. When we're halfway through the ride, you ask the operator to stop the ride. You get off and go somewhere else, to a park attraction that seems more fun to you."

My husband understood my hurt better than any amount of

yelling or accusations could have conveyed. We worked together toward a compromise.

The precious Golden Girls whom I thanked at the beginning of this book were in complete agreement. "Use common sense," I was told again and again. "Don't try and talk to him when he's watchin' a ballgame!" "Get together with your friends when you're lonely, and he's out of town on business. Unload with each other instead of dumping it all on your husband. When he comes home, tell him you appreciate how hard he's working for you." "Show him affection all the time and at unexpected times." Miss Dorothy winked at me. "Those men may act all tough, but they need it too. They eat it up!"

Over and over I heard these women from The Greatest Generation put the best possible face on hard times—long separations, the death of a child, the hard work of getting a business off the ground, multiple miscarriages. The strong thread of togetherness was sewn through every story. For them, as it should be for us, there was no option considered but to stay together.

Remember that you are a team, and you should want to reach a solution that helps *both* of you win.

I remember an old song. I don't suppose you could call it a love song because someone named Jack was exhorted to slip out the back, and Stan was told to make a new plan. Leaving often seems the easy way out. Instead of "50 ways to leave your lover," let's look at 50 ways to love your husband:

1. Buy his favorite ice cream.
2. Shave your legs.
3. Buy satin sheets and initiate a surprise passionate encounter.
4. Brag on him when others can hear you.
5. Pray for him.
6. Keep his confidences.
7. Do the unexpected.
8. Be hospitable to his friends.

9. Pick a day and let him sleep in.

10. Send him a cookie bouquet at work.

11. Wake him in the middle of the night to make love—set the alarm if you have to.

12. Admire his muscles without laughing.

13. View him as if from another woman's eyes.

14. Keep a list of the things he says he wants or would like to do—whenever possible do something from the list for him.

15. Begin to fulfill that list a little at a time.

16. Laugh together, especially at your own private jokes.

17. Rent an old movie. Watch it together in bed with popcorn and cocoa.

18. Take a walk in the rain holding hands.

19. Sleep without your pajamas on.

20. Hold hands as you fall asleep.

21. Send him a love letter in the mail.

22. Tuck one of your lacy bras or a pair of skimpy underwear scented with your perfume into his luggage as a reminder when he goes on an out of town business trip.

23. Spend an afternoon reminiscing about your courtship. Begin to treat him that way again.

24. Watch your wedding video together.

25. Sit in the back row at the movies.

26. Begin a hobby together.

27. Go parking.

28. Go lingerie shopping via catalogue. Let him pick out the things he'd like you to wear.

29. Buy one of the items and wear it!

30. Write his mother a note thanking her for raising such a wonderful son.

31. Place a single rose, or one made of molded chocolate, under his windshield wiper while he's at work.

32. Write an encouraging message on his car window or on the bathroom mirror. Use glass chalk or lipstick.

33. Go on a picnic.

34. Make reservations at a bed and breakfast—kidnap him for the weekend.

35. Buy him a new tie or hunting jacket...present it to him by wearing nothing else.

36. Challenge him to a game of strip checkers.

37. Lose!

38. Do something that makes you feel better about yourself—confidence is sexy!

39. Watch him play with the children and compliment him on being such a good father.

40. Surprise him in the shower.

41. Take a bubble bath together.

42. Fill your bedroom with candles and your bed with rose petals.

43. Subscribe to a special interest magazine that he enjoys.

44. Encourage him to have a guys' night out.

45. Write a list of the top ten things you love about him and leave it on his pillow.

46. Watch him as he drifts off to sleep.

47. Bring him breakfast in bed or make a special breakfast for him before he leaves for work.

48. Put a pair of silk boxers in his dresser drawer.

49. Solicit his opinion on a decision that is usually left up to you and then heed it.

50. Accept him unconditionally.

The Blueprint for a Helpmate

Let's take a trip back to Genesis and look at the foundational plan for marriage. After a chapter and a half of God surveying His wonderful creation and pronouncing it "very good," God sees the first thing that is negative. "The LORD God said, 'It is not good for the man to be alone. I will make a helper suitable for him'" (Genesis 2:18). Forget about a dog supposedly being man's best friend; out of all the wonderful creatures God had thought of and made, "for Adam no suitable helper was found" (Genesis 2:20).

"Then the LORD God made a woman from the rib he had taken out of the man and he brought her to the man. The man said, 'This is now bone of my bones and flesh of my flesh; she shall be called "woman," for she was taken out of man.' For this reason a man will leave his father and mother and be united to his wife, and they will become one flesh" (Genesis 2:22-24).

There is a poignant commentary on this special creation for Adam that is often repeated in wedding ceremonies: Woman was not taken from man's head that she should lord over him, or from his feet to be trampled by him, but from near his side to be equal with him, from under his arm to be protected by him, and from near his heart to be loved by him.

What an honor to have been created especially for your husband. You were, you know. No one else can complete him in the way in which your union has freed you to do. The blueprint God created reveals just how and why we are made for our husbands.

1. Leave

Genesis 2:24 continues, "For this reason a man will leave his father and mother." After marriage are we still to honor our parents? Absolutely. Scripture commands it. "Honor your father and your mother, as the LORD your God has commanded you, *so that* you may live long and that it may go well with you" (Deuteronomy 5:16, emphasis mine).

In the gospel of Matthew, when Jesus is talking to the Pharisees about what is clean and unclean, He tells them that it is not acceptable to say to your father or mother, "Whatever help you might otherwise have received from me is a gift devoted to God" (Matthew 15:5). The Pharisees were using this argument to get out of helping their parents, and it was blatant hypocrisy, a skill at which they were unfortunately gifted.

However, our first priority must still be to our mates. We can gently let parents know that they cannot dictate our time and our schedules. Obviously there may be seasons when a parent is seriously ill, grieving, or incapacitated and needs more care than usual; it is still important to take time to nurture your relationship with your spouse and take needed breaks.

2. Cleave

"And be united to his wife, and they will become one flesh" (Genesis 2:24). The Hebrew connotation means to cling to, hold fast to. As a married couple, you are a unit of one facing the world together. Nothing is to separate that outlook.

The independence the world teaches women has given us the freedom to contract STDs in unprecedented numbers, attract scores of broken hearts and homes, and end the life of any unborn baby found inconvenient. It doesn't sound too impressive.

Now don't get me wrong. I believe women are just as intelligent as men and that we should vote, own property, and be able to work in any career; however, that doesn't mean I think in order to be on top and make it in a man's world, a woman must subvert her feminine qualities and be harsh, brash, and unfeeling. I also don't think that life is an endless competition with men.

As a female high school history and constitutional law teacher, I was often the lone female in the "Great Social Studies Sea of Male Coaches." I never once felt that I was treated in a condescending manner, nor did I dress or behave any differently. If you could have talked to any of the male teachers who were my colleagues during those years, I think they would have said that we enjoyed a mutual respect for one another. Were there coaches who tended to put athletics above academia? Sure. But I met just as many teachers who were motivating their classes by using uniquely male approaches that perhaps reached a different type of student than I could best reach. We often joked about the stereotypes in teacher meetings.

And if you keep hearing that we are the same as men except for our sex organs, don't you believe it! We *are* different than men and it's by design. God's design. In *general* men are stronger, taller, and bigger than women. Men's brains are larger, but women's have more brain cells. (Sadly, I think we lose some with the birth of every child!) Men tend to think compartmentally better than women and they may use intelligence and thought processing to excel at different skills or reach different conclusions. And that's not coming close to describing all of it!

3. Unite

Ecclesiastes 4:9-12 is often quoted in wedding ceremonies. "Two are better than one, because they have a good return for their work: If one falls down, his friend can help him up. But pity the man who falls and has no one to help him up! Also, if two lie down together, they will keep warm. But how can one keep warm alone? Though one may be overpowered, two can defend themselves. A cord of three strands is not quickly broken."

What a beautiful word picture of marital friendship. It's a partnership. Whether your roles are traditional, or you have a job outside the home, or occasionally help mow the lawn during a crazy week, you are both contributing something exceedingly valuable to your home, your children, your community, God's kingdom, and each other.

Be honest. Isn't it wonderful to place your freezing feet against warm, manly legs at night? It's a blessing to have a strong protector who will make you feel safe, give you his jacket when you get cold at the movies, and gets up to check for prowlers when you hear that weird noise—again. The word "cord" brings to mind an intertwined braiding of rope. It's strong. It's harder to fray. When God is added to this cord, it takes a lot of tugging to break it. It's not impossible though, so be diligent about caring for your marriage.

Interdependence is a great model of a biblical concept: mutual submission. Ephesians 5:21 says, "Submit to one another out of reverence for Christ." The reason we are to submit cannot be missed. We do it because of who Christ is and because He asked us to do it.

Let's do a quick attitude check. "A man walked into a library and asked the librarian for a copy of the book *Man the Master of Woman.* Without looking up she pointed and said, 'Sir, the fiction is in that corner.'"[8] Is that your attitude about submission? About surrendering yourself to your husband's God-ordained leadership? Cheerfully accepting his decisions as long as they don't go against God's will?

4. Be Fruitful and Multiply

This was God's original directive to all living things. God said it again to Noah and his sons after every living thing was destroyed in the flood (Genesis 9:1). Of course it was intended to increase the population of the earth, but at the heart of the matter was family. And at the heart of family is marriage. It is the foundational unit of life and it's no coincidence that God uses imagery of both marriage and family throughout the Bible. We are called the bride of Christ and the family of God. Being fruitful also bears the connotation of accomplishing something together, leaving a lasting and formidable legacy. I can think of no better legacy than a forever marriage and children whom you have influenced to be strong godly leaders, marriage partners, and parents in their own right someday.

5. Stay

For how long? Well, forever. Until you are separated by death. "I quit" are the two most devastating words you can use in a marriage. Strike them from your vocabulary and pray diligently about striking them from your thoughts.

As a very little girl I remember hearing the refrain of an old country song that played sometimes on the radio when I was riding in the car with my parents. It spoke about not wanting to play house...the little girl in the song didn't like that game because what she saw of it only involved pain and separation. I always thought that it was a haunting song and now, as a wife and mother, I am always thrilled when "house" is my girls' game of choice.

Marriage is intended to be much more serious than just a promise in the way we understand a promise. It is a *covenant* relationship. The word "covenant" is serious business in Bible speak. The Hebrew word *berith* is usually translated *covenant*. It can also mean treaty, strong agreement, allies or allied, but *covenant* is still the favored meaning. The Old Testament contains that Hebrew word 285 times! The Old Testament itself is referred to as the tablets of the *berith,* or the tablets of the *covenant*.

Covenant relationships are often accompanied by a sign. In Genesis chapter nine, God initiates a covenant with Noah, a pledge never again to destroy the earth with flooding. The sign of that promise is a rainbow. We remember that covenant each time we see it.

Covenants sometimes involved a promise to keep on both sides. In Genesis chapter 17, when Abram was 99 years old, God speaks to him. "I will establish my covenant as an everlasting covenant between me and you and your descendants after you...I will give [the land of Canaan] as an everlasting possession to you and your descendants after you; and I will be their God" (verses 7-8). Abram's part in this covenant was to undergo circumcision and to circumcise every male at eight days old in the generations to come. It was a sign, a symbol of the promise.

Most likely, in your wedding ceremony you exchanged two sets of vows, one of which involved the exchanging of rings. The minister mentioned that the rings were made of a durable and precious metal and that they were fashioned in an unending circle, symbolizing a lasting and permanent union. Next time you have your wedding rings cleaned or glance down at them, let them remind you of this covenant.

When Jacob took his family and possessions and snuck away from his treacherous father-in-law, Laban, there was an ugly confrontation a few days later when Laban and a group of his relatives caught up with them. Even though Laban does not admit his wrongdoing, he suggests making a covenant with Jacob.

"So Jacob took a stone and set it up as a monument. Then he told his family members, 'Gather some stones.' So they gathered stones and piled them in a heap. Then Jacob and Laban sat down beside the pile of stones to eat a covenant meal. To commemorate the event, Laban called the place Jegar-sahadutha (which means 'witness pile' in Aramaic), and Jacob called it Galeed (which means 'witness pile' in Hebrew). Then Laban declared, 'This pile of stones will stand as a witness to remind us of the covenant we have made today.'...But it was also called Mizpah (which means 'watchtower'), for Laban said, 'May the LORD keep watch between us to make sure that we keep this covenant when we are out of each other's sight'" (Genesis 31:45-49 NLT).

Although Laban suggested this "witness pile" because of his mistrust, I'd like to suggest that you make a different sort of *Galeed* with your husband. Consider one of these ideas:

- ♥ Fill a beautiful jar with sand or seashells from your honeymoon site.

- ♥ Tie a band of twigs with ribbon or stack beautiful rocks from the mountain cabin in which you stayed on an anniversary retreat.

- ♥ Make a shadow box of wedding mementoes—a napkin, your engraved invitation, a favorite picture, a scrap of lace, some dried petals from your bouquet, and his boutonniere.

Let it serve as a "witness pile," a visible reminder in your home. It will be a sign of the covenant you made to each other in front of witnesses and God Himself.

In fact three states, Arkansas, Arizona, and Louisiana, currently offer something known as covenant marriage. Couples choosing this option agree to premarital counseling and divorce is much harder to obtain. Just cause is typically limited to abuse, a felony conviction with jail time, or adultery.

Dedicate your pile asking God, not from a spirit of mistrust, but from hearts that long to stay the course, to keep watch over you and help you guard your covenant when you are away from each other. Pray for each other and your marriage each time you pass it.

Dr. Kevin Leman has founded an organization known as Couples of Promise. The first of what he calls The Ten Commitments is perhaps the most indispensable: "We commit ourselves to make love a daily choice, *even when life looks easier somewhere else.*"[9] The emphasis is mine because we all know that it will sometimes look easier somewhere else. But if you hang on, you'll find that what lies beneath is the rich soil that makes the blooming possible.

CHOCOLATE-COVERED QUESTIONS

1. What specific symptoms of *pigitis* can you identify in yourself?

2. What items can we use to build our "witness pile"? Prepare a special covenant meal and eat it to dedicate your own *Galeed*.

3. Read the Genesis 2 blueprint. What, if anything, jumped out at you this time?

4. Caution: Make sure you work through this question during a relaxed time when you aren't feeling confrontational or irritated with each other. Sometimes we badger our husbands, or we mother them (and they already have one of those!), or we nag them (even though we may call it gently reminding) and are surprised and hurt when they ignore our requests or respond rudely. Below is a list of selected statements from John Gray's classic book *Men Are from Mars, Women Are from Venus*. First, read the list on your own to see if any of these sound like you. (Yes, it's painful.) Second, have your husband read the list and circle the five statements that you really do say—those that annoy him the most. Third, think of a different way you could approach your request and place a * by the items that you could just graciously overlook (see my notes on the Big Deal Scale, p. 44). Fourth, check with your husband to make sure your alternate approaches would be acceptable.

   1. How can you think of buying that? You already have one.

   2. Those dishes are still wet. They'll dry with spots.

   3. Your hair is getting kind of long, isn't it?

   4. There's a parking spot over there. Turn around.

   5. You want to spend time with your friends. What about me?

   6. Don't put that there. It will get lost.

   7. You should call a plumber. He'll know what to do.

8. Why are we waiting for a table? Didn't you make reservations?

9. Your office is still a mess. How can you think in here? When are you going to clean it up?

10. I didn't know where you were. (You should have called.)

11. Those potato chips are too greasy. They're not good for your heart.

12. Bill called for the third time. When are you going to call him back? [10]

SCRIPTURE

"So they are no longer two, but one. Therefore what God has joined together, let man not separate" (Matthew 19:6).

HOT CHOCOLATE TOPIC

How can I be a better helpmate to you and for you?

GOODNIGHT KISS

Today I choose to love you.

WHAT DO YOU THINK YOUR MOM AND DAD HAVE IN COMMON?

Both don't want any more kids.

LORI, AGE 8

4

Communicating in Chocolate
Breaking the Code

Remember a sense of humor does not mean that you
tell him jokes, it means that you laugh at his.

UNKNOWN

After a steady diet of Gary Smalley, James Dobson, and a host of other communication experts, I felt armed for anything—even the task of transforming my reticent husband into the only effusive male communicator this side of *Star Trek*. Trouble is, as my wise sister pointed out, because men *are* from Mars, they won't read the book! Alas, I concluded that there really are some places in marital conversation that we should just leave things be. If we accept certain ideas as absolutes, it could save us a lot of heartache and relationship damage.

For instance, one should never expect a husband to ask directions to anywhere, regardless of how brief the amount of time left before you are expected to arrive at a destination or the preponderance of hours spent wandering aimlessly. (Be not fooled, GPS and Mapquest notwithstanding, it still happens.) My husband does not like to refer to this activity as "lost." He prefers to call it the "scenic route" or the beloved "shortcut."

In fact, a direct question as to our whereabouts leads to a much longer trip in proportion to the number of times I discreetly inquire, "How much longer do you think, dear?" Instead of asking, I now simply plead an incredibly urgent need for a bathroom stop at the nearest store. Crouching low in front of the counter, I just hiss at the clerk and beg for directions. Upon emerging from the store, I pretend to suddenly spot a familiar landmark (it makes absolutely no difference if we haven't been in that state before) and away we go! Even if your man is directionally challenged, he's smart enough to play along if you're smart enough to pretend that he's forging the path.

Breaking the Code

My typically verbal husband is rendered speechless by the phrase, "let's talk." The mere thought of spending an evening chatting about everything, and yet nothing in particular, drives most men insane.

Greg wants an agenda, a specific line item to talk about. So in a pathetic attempt to be more accommodating, I wrote out daily joys, grievances, and financial concerns alphabetically and by topic and presented them for our conversing pleasure. He dispatched the entire list in under five minutes, listing neat solutions in the right hand column. Then we sat staring at each other. Finally I surrendered to meaningful, but spontaneous, bursts of conversation in between diapering, carpooling the kindergartner, and prying stuck Cheerios out of our youngest daughter's hair. It was better than nothing. And apparently he was even listening during these on the fly exchanges because a few weeks later, after a lively discussion on the value of romance and subtlety as a prelude to intimacy, Greg dumped half a box of Calgon on me in the bathtub. It was a start.

Then the really good stuff—he came home from work bearing a Snickers bar and a beautiful bouquet of flowers. Only a few of the blooms bore the marks of briefcase rivets. He entered the living room looking boyishly shy and endearing. I, however, was deeply engrossed in a book. (I think the title may have been something like *Discovering Your Husband's Secret Desires*.) The crinkled edges of a candy bar wrapper brushed the back of my neck. I batted Greg's hand away and scrunched up my shoulders.

"Get a life," I muttered dismissively.

"I was trying to be flirtatious."

"Oh." I put down my book. "Why didn't you say so?" So much for subtlety. I'm thinking of hanging a sign and attaching a marker to it to indicate desire levels: "oh yeah!" "thinking about it," or "not a chance."

My husband is Mr. Steady. Not me. The graciousness of my mood depends on how good my hair looks and whether or not I'm having a bad body day. I've yet to hear a man complain of either of these conditions. But every female in my acquaintance owns a slimming black outfit for such an occasion. I wore mine three times last week.

"What's with you?" my husband inquired innocently. "Are you in mourning for something?"

"As a matter of fact, I am," I snapped. "I am mourning the disappearance of my B.C. body and the way the drycleaners continue to shrink my clothes!"

"B.C. body?" he ventured.

I rolled my eyes. "Before children." And don't get me started on how men age with distinction and we just age.

"You cannot do a kindness too soon,
For you never know how soon it will be too late."

RALPH WALDO EMERSON

The despair caused by any topic under discussion grows incrementally larger according to the lateness of the hour. Some of our best fights about really important things like the circumference of the largest dust bunny under the refrigerator or who ate the last bowl of chocolate mint ice cream have been after ten o'clock.

It's an abhorrent waste of sleep, but for some reason there's another topic we can't let go. The two of us will be lying in bed, securely cuddled and just about to drift off when one of us will ask, "Did you?"

"Why are you asking me?" the other retorts defensively. "Since when did we decide that door checking is *my* job?"

If it's my night to be the askee rather than the asker, I have to admit to an unfortunate tendency to pout. After climbing back into bed, I release a long-suffering sigh and cling tightly to the box springs on my side of the bed, making sure that no part of me is touching my husband. He always falls for this. "What's wrong, honey?"

"Nothing," is my standard reply. And because he is a member of that intriguing male species, he has the audacity to believe me. Either that or he has broken my code and knows better than to challenge me in that particular mood.

Maybe it's not necessary to be on the same wavelength. One day I accosted my unsuspecting husband just as he entered the yard. I waved a garden spade in one hand and a three pound bag of mulch in the other. My knees, gardening gloves, and hair were full of dirt. I pointed excitedly to my planted row of flowers. "Aren't they beautiful?"

He stared at the spectacle before him and said, "Don't hug me."

Unfazed, I bubbled, "I'm just as happy as a clam!"

"How happy *are* clams, honey? Really."

"Plenty happy. They make pearls...or is that oysters?"

He patted my head. "I'm just happy that you're happy." He's a very smart man.

We've made progress. One night after an especially precious evening together, I was feeling sentimental. "Honey," I began, "I have something really important to tell you and I want you to be serious." He made a variety of comic faces as I rattled off my heartfelt appreciation for our passion and friendship. When I finished, he threw back his head and gave one of his rare guffaws.

Determined to be the gracious one, I stretched and smiled smugly. "I'll just take your immature response as proof that you're so overcome with emotion that your masculine ego won't allow you to respond." I heard him chuckle.

But I'm content with that. Really. I've accepted our differences, and though I'll always be a Dobson fan, I'm through trying to change my husband into a poster man for stellar communication. It's actually kind of fascinating to try and interpret those grunts, groans, and

Prepare DCD Brownie Mix and DCD Mousse following directions on package.

Stir together the packet of spiced Chai tea and a container of Cool Whip.

When Brownies are cooled, cut into 2 inch squares. Place 1/3 of Brownies in the bottom of a Trifle bowl.

Add 1/3 Mousse.

Add 1/3 Chai Cool Whip

Add 1/3 fruit

Layer till all items are used.

Take DCD Dark Chocolate and sprinkle shavings on top.

Refrigerate till time to serve.

DCD TRIFLE

DCD Mouse Mix
4 oz. DCD Dark Chocolate (2 bars)
¾ cup Heavy Cream
DCD Truffle Fudge Brownie Mix
1 Stick Butter
2 Large Eggs
1 Packet DCD Spiced Chai Tea
1 Tub Cool Whip
Favorite Fruit
DCD Dark Chocolate (1 bar) - shavings

enigmatic expressions. Except just once I'd like for him...well...not goin' there. It's enough for *me* to know the truth.

The Oreo Factor

Sometimes in order to get to the good fluffy stuff inside (especially if it's double stuff), you have to twist and crack the hard cookie edges. This is true of the harder issues in a marriage too. Yeah, we know how to talk—we can even listen on occasion. But it is a rare and wonderful thing in a relationship when a couple sends and receives the same message.

Men tend to be straightforward in communicating desires, goals, and solutions. Women, at least most of us, operate with a set of hidden agendas and expectations, often without meaning to. We can be spilling our guts to our husbands over burgers and fries at a quaint fifties diner downtown and they can, without missing a beat, eye the remaining fries on our plate and inquire, "So are you gonna eat those?" What gives?

And of course, there's the undisputed fact that most of us are more emotional than our male counterparts. Most of the chapters you're reading underwent scrutiny for typos and clarity by several different people. In the margin next to one moving story, a woman had written, "I cried." The male reader wrote next to that, "I intellectually analyzed the content." I laughed when I read both comments, recognizing both humor and the clear difference between how we handle what moves us.

Differences in our communication styles carry over to our problem solving styles. In a study of one-year-old children "a barrier was placed between the child and his or her mother. The boys, wanting to get back to Mommy, try to get around or over the barrier or they try to knock it down...The female children, on the other hand, verbalized their distress, and their mommies came and picked them up."[1]

Can you see the difference in how we seek to resolve a problem compared to our husbands? Their solution is physical—they want to fix it. To knock the problem down. To hold us. To change the oil. To repair the steps. To work out a solution. Our solution is to process the situation verbally. The problem with our method can be that we sometimes talk a problem to death, and sometimes we cause our husbands to feel inadequate because we don't allow them to do what they were born to do.

Noted marriage researcher Dr. John Gottman says, "In order to fully understand why husbands and wives so often miss each other's needs, we have to recognize that the sexes may be physically programmed to react differently to emotional conflict—beginning in childhood."[2]

In *The Wonder of Boys,* author Michael Gurian explains eight different internal processing methods of expressing feelings and emotions. I've chosen two that I think capture the biggest ongoing differences in our processing styles, even when boys become men.

> Men often use an active-release approach; they sort through feelings by engaging in an aggressive game of basketball, lifting a few weights, going for a run, yelling.
>
> A second common response is the suppression-delayed method. You and I process verbally, perhaps even talking aloud to ourselves if there isn't anyone else to direct our comments or rants! But since men are more goal-oriented they often delay emotional reactions until the problem is solved.[3]

Knowing this, it's unreasonable for us to expect that *while* we are on the side of the road with a flat tire in freezing temperatures, he will be telling us all about how he feels! We can be thankful for that. After he changes the tire, gets back in the car, and thaws out, *then* he'll probably say, "Well that was fun."

If we don't understand this glaring difference, we may forget to encourage our men because we mistakenly believe they don't *have* any feelings. Encouragement is a vital part of communication and relationship.

Men confront to problem solve; women "confront to connect."[4] When we come to our husbands and say, "Honey, can we talk?" their first thought is often, "Uh oh, what am I in trouble for now?" Try to make your talk times pleasant and productive, not laying blame.

We tend to mistake the silence of their processing (it's slower than ours, but can yield some amazing insights) for reticence or the absence of an opinion, so we rush in and flood the silence with talking. The Living Bible expresses Proverbs 10:19 this way: "Don't talk so much. You keep putting your foot in your mouth. Be sensible and turn off the flow!" Perhaps we would do well to keep the faucet off and not let it run until we've given our spouse his turn to talk, however long that takes.

"A quick note for husbands: When your wife comes across as complaining, controlling, or disrespectful, she is often crying out, 'Love me!' Look past her behavior for her heart."[5]

ADAPTED FROM EMERSON EGGERICHS IN *LOVE AND RESPECT*

General studies show that women use approximately twice as many words per day as do men. Her 50,000 word quota compared to his 25,000 word usage can set up a small world of problems because we women often spend a lot of wasted time trying to badger, pull, prod, and harangue communication out of our men. Believe me, communication extracted from a man in this manner isn't going to be useful or satisfying.

Besides the actual word count discrepancy, studies show that women are more likely to accompany their words with gestures and five tones while men tend to use fewer gestures and only three tones.[6]

Girls also speak earlier than boys, mastering language with relative ease, and generally have a longer word quota throughout their lives. When my youngest three ranged from infant to preschooler, I met my girlfriends Tammy and Amy to walk in the mall twice a week. I had three verbal, vocalizing girls; Tammy and Amy both had boys. Unbeknownst to me, my precious friend Tammy took her son Aaron to the pediatrician because she was concerned about how relatively nonverbal he was in comparison to the girls. When the doctor explained these core differences to her, Tammy conspiratorially told me, "Some things never change."

> *Try whispering in your sweetheart's left ear.*
> *Sam Houston State University researchers have*
> *discovered that emotional requests are better*
> *understood when they're spoken into the left ear.*
> *That's the side controlled by the right brain where*
> *emotional and creative stimuli are processed.*
> WOMAN'S WORLD, JUNE 2004 ISSUE

Levels of Communication

There are five basic levels of communication. When you recognize these levels, they can help you gauge your connection and intimacy. While good communication can lead to a good relationship, bad communication is a symptom of a relationship's struggles.

Level Five: Cliché Conversation

"Hi, how are you?" "Beautiful weather we're having." "Nice suit." "What are you doing for the holidays?" It's pleasant, but it's without depth, and it's not enough to maintain a relationship.

Level Four: Reporting Facts About Others

It is easy for marriages with young children to fall into a level four rut. "Don't forget that Jenny has piano lessons today." "I need you to run this by the bank for me." "The baby's poop is a weird color, don't you think?" "Jim got Sharon the most beautiful diamond bracelet for their anniversary!" "The bank at Fourth and Main got robbed last night."

Level Three: Ideas and Judgments

This level reaches on tiptoe to touch the edge of true communication. We share ideas, thoughts, opinions, likes, dislikes. Dating conversation hovers here as we guardedly offer our thoughts on everything from country music to Italian cuisine.

Level Two: Feelings and Emotions

We women like to hang out here, don't we! I rarely have difficulty sharing or explaining how I feel about something, regardless of the topic. Men prefer to circumvent this with action. My dad used to share this illustration:

> A man and his wife were sitting at the breakfast table as was their usual habit. He was absorbed in reading the newspaper and his wife was longing for conversation. "Honey," she asked timidly, "do you love me?"
>
> He glanced at her over the top of the paper. "I told you that I loved you when I married you. If I ever change my mind, I'll let you know."

Don't expect your husband to be a mind reader. It sounds so romantic to believe "If he loved me, he'd just know what I want," but trust me, this doesn't work. You'll save yourself lots of frustration if you'll just tell your husband what you'd like. On gift giving occasions I give Greg a list of options to choose from. By doing it this way I get to keep the element of surprise that I crave. He's even asked me to keep a folder full of ideas or items circled in catalogs so that when he wants to surprise me, he'll have some idea about what I'm wanting!

Just keep in mind that, to a man, the way he provides for you and the things he does for you are most likely his most natural expressions of love.

Level One: Complete Emotional and Personal Truthfulness

What makes this level so lovely, so rare, and so *hard,* is that it contains words like transparency, honesty, vulnerability. To a certain degree, all of us feel a reluctance to bare our souls. Most men have an even greater struggle with this, particularly since we live in a society that constantly urges men to "suck it up," "take it like a man," or "don't show weakness." However, it is worth creating the atmosphere in which this kind of talking can thrive on a regular basis because it is not possible for a marriage to survive without this depth.[7]

It's important to note that men can be more straightforward than we are inclined to be...they generally say what they mean. We need to stop looking for subtext. States Susan Heitler, a Denver-based clinical psychologist, "Whenever partners guess, rather than ask, each other's thoughts, they usually assume the worst-case scenario."[8] I've found this to be true. It's fairly safe to assume that women get most of our marital exercise by jumping to conclusions. We're frequently guilty of thinking we know what our spouse is going to say before we give them a chance to finish their thought.

That Nagging Problem

H. Norman Wright, during a talk on communication in marriage, reminded me of what I'd forgotten since my college day classes in psychology, sociology, and counseling. There are actually six different things people can hear during communication:

1. What you meant to say

2. What you actually said

3. What the other person heard

4. What the other person *thought* he heard

5. What the other person will say about what you said

6. What you *think* the other person said about what you said

Whew! Anybody else besides me almost scared to say anything else? Whenever we cast the most negative light on our spouses, the usual results are resentment and nagging. We contract a bad case of martyr syndrome, and it's highly contagious! The nagging problem in your marriage just might be your nagging.

Karol Ladd, in her book *The Power of a Positive Wife*, exposes what nagging may be composed of:

1. Repeating a command or demand more than once

2. Using a disrespectful or whiny tone

3. Huffing off when he doesn't do what you want him to do

4. Grumbling and complaining aloud or under your breath

5. Standing over him with your arms crossed, tapping your big toe on the floor, or wagging your pointer finger in his face

6. Giving the silent treatment[9]

Not only does nagging sound bad, it fails to accomplish the very things we were hoping for. Most men need to feel in control and will resist being hounded into doing something. Even if it makes perfect sense, ideas and projects are often rejected if presented in the wrong manner.

Although I am a big fan of women's groups—Girls Night Out, MOPS, Bible Study, Book Clubs, or informal get-togethers—make sure that your gatherings don't turn into a griping, man-bashing session. This is not the place for airing private, marital grievances or for sharing deeply personal secrets that belong only between husband and wife. Keep your most intimate exchanges private. Your husband will stop sharing with you if you're sharing his dreams, insecurities, and concerns with others. You would feel the same hurt if you discovered that he was telling his coworkers or male friends about your personal matters.

It is a wise wife who limits information that could hurt her husband and confines her tattling on him to her conversations with God. However, feel free to talk him up and compliment your husband to others all you want! When it gets back to him, and it will, you have planted a seed of encouragement that may grow into a full grown tree.

Communicating about time issues is another sore spot in marriage. Authors Wendy and David Hubbert feel that most couples are a combination of Time-Crammers and Time-Underestimators. One of you (the Time Crammer) waits until the last minute, filling the time with "just one more task" until before you know it, the ideal departure time has passed.

A Time-Underestimator, on the other hand, truly believes she will be ready to go on time, it's just that time has such a vague meaning. David Hubbert offers this chart (of which he says men everywhere are in agreement) as a means of translating his wife's time estimates into real time:

- ♥ Just a second = 10 minutes
- ♥ 5 minutes = 30 minutes
- ♥ 15 minutes = 1 hour
- ♥ Half an hour = Find a good book
- ♥ Hold your horses = 5-minute penalty
- ♥ You're annoying me = 10-minute penalty
- ♥ Just go without me = If you do, I'll kill you[10]

Furthermore, as far as communication goes, the strong, silent type in the movies has been vastly overrated. I'm married to one of those types. He's a cop. He can, and has, interrogated suspects for hours, but isn't usually as willing to spill that many words with me. Maybe I should just be grateful that he isn't interrogating me!

Conflict Differences

For both small and large decisions, and if you're really new at this or in a deep rut, it is good to have a neutral, concrete way of voicing and comparing your opinions on an issue. Marriage therapists and authors Les and Leslie Parrott have designed conflict cards for just such situations. The cards use a scale, from one to ten, ranking the intensity of a person's feelings:

1. "I'm not enthusiastic, but it's no big deal to me."
2. "I don't see it the way you do, but I may be wrong."
3. "I don't agree, but I can live with it."
4. "I don't agree, but I'll let you have your way."
5. "I don't agree and cannot remain silent on this."
6. "I do not approve, and I need more time."
7. "I strongly disapprove and cannot go along with it."
8. "I will be so seriously upset, I can't predict my reaction."
9. "No possible way! If you do, I quit!"
10. "Over my dead body!"[11]

When you're deciding whether or not to move the family to Vermont or let a set of in-laws move in with you for the summer, you might discover that it's a two for one of you, but a seven for the other. Both of you can literally lay your cards on the table, letting the varying numbers speak for themselves. The Parrotts say that in heated discussions, this method helps "level the playing field."

You're already familiar with substituting the accusatory "you" statements (you always...you never) for "I" statements (this makes me feel like I...), however, you might not know to pay attention to how often you use the word "but" as a disclaimer. That word can be inflammatory when it prefaces every response to something the other partner says. The next time you are tempted to use the standby disclaimer, choose "and" or "at the same time." "Believe it or not, this simple substitution is one of the quickest ways to convert a prickly conversation into a smooth one." [12]

Whenever you add something new to your communication skill repertoire, it may feel awkward or uncomfortable, but that's a good thing. It means you're breaking your old habits and replacing them with valuable knowledge.

Lots of chocolates to you as you spend time talking—and listening—to your sweetheart today.

Chocolate-Covered Questions

1. Back when I was in high school, students circulated a sheet of paper containing an anonymous work called "The Rules."

The Rules

1. The Female always makes the Rules.

2. The Rules are subject to change at any time without prior notification.

3. No Male can possibly know all the Rules.

4. If the Female suspects the Male knows all the Rules, she must immediately change some or all of the Rules.

5. The Female is NEVER wrong.

6. If the Female is wrong, it is because of a flagrant misunderstanding which was a direct result of something the Male did or said wrong.

7. If Rule 6 applies, the Male must apologize immediately for causing the misunderstanding.

8. The Female can change her mind at any given point in time.

9. The Male must never change his mind without written consent from the Female.

10. The Female has every right to be angry or upset at any given time.

11. The Male must remain calm at all times, unless the Female wants him to be angry or upset.

12. The Female must under NO CIRCUMSTANCES let the Male know whether or not she wants him to be angry or upset.

13. Any attempt to document these Rules could result in bodily harm.

14. If the Female has PMS, all the Rules are null and void.

Most of us will chuckle a bit because there is some truth in those "rules." However, each rule violates God's rules for governing our relationship. Which of these unofficial "rules" do you feel like you most often invoke? What is your husband's answer? What Scriptures do you know that refute these rules? Together come up with at least four.

2. Why do you think timing is so important in communication?

3. Would you say your spouse *hears* you or *listens* to you? Why? Tell your spouse two concrete things that you could do to improve your listening skills.

4. Which method of communicating does each of you feel works best for you? Why? What's the middle ground of compromise?

5. Which of the five levels of communication below do you feel that you and your spouse spend most of your talk time in? Where do you want to be? What would best help change that?

- ♥ Cliché conversation

- ♥ Reporting facts

- ♥ Ideas and judgments

- ♥ Feelings and emotions

- ♥ Complete emotional and personal truthfulness

SCRIPTURE

"A word aptly spoken is like apples of gold in settings of silver"
(Proverbs 25:11).

HOT CHOCOLATE TOPIC

Do you agree that women talk more than men? How good do you think you are at handling our different communication styles? How could you improve?

GOODNIGHT KISS

Honey, I pledge to listen to your point of view before jumping to conclusions. I'll find a new form of exercise.

WHAT DO MOST PEOPLE DO ON A DATE?

Dates are for having fun, and people should use them to get to know each other. Even boys have something to say if you listen long enough.

LYNNETTE, AGE 8

"Carob is a brown powder made from the pulverized fruit of a Mediterranean evergreen. Some consider carob an adequate substitute for chocolate because it has some similar nutrients (calcium, phosphorus), and because it can, when combined with vegetable fat and sugar, be made to approximate the color and consistency of chocolate. Of course, the same arguments can as persuasively be made in favor of dirt."

SANDRA BOYNTON

Sharing Chocolate
Doing Life Together

Chains do not hold a marriage together. It is threads, hundreds of tiny threads, which sew people together through the years.

SIMONE SIGNORET

It's our own fault really. Living in a harlequin-wrapped world, dining on romantic sitcoms capable of neatly solving all problems of family life in half-hour intervals, allotting six minutes for commercial breaks—it's no wonder we women have such a skewed view of romance! Let me tell you about something that once happened to cause me to revamp my definition of romance.

I never dreamed my faith in my husband's romance quotient would be restored the night the septic tank exploded. I was in the combination utility room/downstairs bathroom completing my nightly routine—throwing in one last load of laundry before heading upstairs to bed—when I heard it. It was an odd rumbling sound growing in intensity and volume. It sounded like a wicked combination of caffeinated cowboys, drunken dragons, and starved lions was viciously battling it out.

With difficulty I turned my eight months pregnant body from the washer and dryer platform toward the source of the sounds, the toilet. The sounds grew ominous. Gingerly

I lifted the lid and a part of life that I generally spend time avoiding, literally hit the (ceiling) fan.

Shrieking, I bolted from the room hysterically calling my husband's name. "Greg! Oh, Greg. Oh, no. I really need you!" He flew around the corner, anticipating a premature trip to the hospital. My hands covered my mouth in horror as I pointed toward the bathroom. A brown geyser was spurting from the toilet to the ceiling. Other water of varying colors was overflowing the bowl and quickly flooding the floor. The stench was hideous.

I ran for the phone to call a 24 hour septic service. By the time they answered, my husband had already gone outside and removed the lid of the clean out valve, allowing the pressure to release somewhere other than in the house.

I lowered my awkward bulk to the kitchen floor and sobbed. "Go to bed, sweetheart. You can't help me and I really don't want you around all those chemicals anyway," Greg said. I shook my head vehemently—I wanted to help.

"The biggest help you could be would be to go to bed. I can't deal with this and you." At my crestfallen look, he bent and kissed the tip of my nose.

I trudged upstairs and pressed my nose against the glass panes of our bedroom window. In the moonlight I saw my husband make trip after trip, mop and buckets in hand, out to the farthest acre to dump his...ur...fertilizer, and return again and again. This was one quirk of the crazy old farmhouse we'd been restoring that I couldn't cope with. Eventually, I lay down and cried myself to sleep.

In the morning I tiptoed downstairs. I walked through each room, the acrid smell of fresh bleach assailing my nostrils. I wrinkled my nose, but curiosity got the best of me so I headed for the utility room. My eyes widened as I took in the sight. There was not a sign of water, silt, or that other stuff anywhere!

The bathroom gleamed. A brand-new mop and bucket stood guard by the pedestal sink and new bathmats and a toilet cover graced the floor and throne, courtesy of my husband and the Wal-Mart Supercenter.

Greg quietly walked up and stood beside me. He whispered in my ear, "Did I do alright, honey? Everything seem okay to you?" I turned and flung my arms around his neck in gratitude.

Moments later, ready to leave for school, I backed down the long gravel drive, carefully looking in the rearview mirror. Reflected there, I saw further evidence of true love. In blue glass chalk, my husband had drawn a gigantic heart on the back window of the minivan. In backward letters so they would read correctly in the mirror were the letters GD + CD = True Love Forever.

Perhaps like me, you need to rethink your definition of romance. Growing up, my sister and I were always hounding our daddy to live life the way we thought it was meant to be lived. Be romantic—get Mom some flowers, take her to dinner, and buy her surprises! He usually ignored us.

But after his death from cancer at the young age of 56, we noticed something was missing from Mom's life—real romance. For 34 years my mother had never filled her car with gasoline or washed or vacuumed it. She had *never* once driven to work or back home on snowy roads; Daddy had always done it for her. Romance? You bet!

Dangerous Drifts

One of the biggest threats to doing life together is an innocuous little something called marital drift. And while sex and money still rank as the top two on the conflict scale, it's the drifting apart that can eventually sink a marriage.

"Drifting sounds painless. Pleasant even. I can almost hear the soft slapping of the waves against the boat; feel the sun kissing water drenched skin and warming my hair. But drifting, by definition, means there is no set course. You're going nowhere. The boat stagnates; the course is eroded by the drip, drip, drip of juggling jobs, kids, electric bills, school, and church obligations and chores."[1]

Think you might be stalled? Drifting? Take this quick, check-up quiz. Answer each question with a "Yes" or "No."

? During the past month have you and your spouse...

❏ kissed passionately without making love?

❏ gone on a date alone? (Double dates or church activities don't count.)

❏ held hands?

❏ talked at length about anything other than the kids, money, schedules, household needs, or conflicts?

❏ done something unexpected, special, or romantic for each other?

❏ prayed together other than at mealtimes?

? During the last six months have you and your spouse...

❏ gone for a long walk together?

❏ laughed until your sides hurt?

❏ taken inventory and discussed your "state of the marital union"?

❏ written a love note or sent a card to each other?

❏ varied your love making in some way—position, technique, location?

? In the last year have you and your spouse...

❏ gone away for an overnight retreat without the kids?

❏ shared a spiritual growth experience?

❏ attended a seminar or read a book to improve your marriage?

❏ shared hopes, goals, fears, and dreams about your marriage and family for the next year, five years, ten years?

❏ verbally renewed your commitment to love and cherish each other and stick it out until you are parted by death?

❓ Scoring

If you responded...

YES to 12 or more questions, you still feel emotionally connected and in love—crank it up a notch to feel even closer.

YES to between 5 and 11 questions, you may have begun settling for an "average" marriage. Implement some good changes.

YES to fewer than 5 questions, your marriage is in serious drift mode and headed for a stall. Start practicing the things on this list and in this book. If you're struggling with very serious issues, consider going to a dedicated Christian counselor for a season.

There's another factor that influences how we live together. I know this will come as a shock to you, but men and women are different! In fact, *Time* magazine reported this little known fact on the cover of one of their magazines! Aside from differences in breathing and heart rates (our hearts beat faster), stress responses, X and Y chromosomes, and the usual stuff, men list their needs differently than we do.

On the survey men where asked, "What is the one thing you'd say you are most seeking from your wife?" Their responses ranged from "Appreciation" to "Sex. Did you really have to ask?" to "Keeping better order around the house."

Here is a key bit of wisdom about our differences: Companionship is to men what conversation is to women. Men were enthusiastic in their answers to questions about that. "Go hunting with me!" "Try golfing with me." "Watch me referee." "Hang out with me." "Attend more public functions and work events with me." "Play Trivial Pursuit." The variety of answers all had one thing in common—a plea to spend time with him. One reason that companionship is so important is because we are giving time that we can't get back. The gift of our undivided, focused attention is always sacrificial and always welcome.

There's no escaping it—shared activity has to be present in a marriage that seeks to be vibrant and thriving. Unfortunately, complaining about lack of sleep, spending habits, and how poorly the Knicks are doing don't really count as shared activities. What to do? It's tough to find common interests, let alone the time to do them! How to compromise? How to get out of a rut? What about all those plain, boring, daily days?

> *Live deep instead of fast.*
> HENRY SEIDEL CANBY

Time Crunch—It's Not a Snack!

We tend to think that because we are living together, we *are* doing life together, but it's not really the same thing at all. Current lifestyles dictate that homes are turning into hotels. What we really need is the intimacy, pace, and atmosphere of a bed and breakfast, not a hotel.

We're too busy.

Marriage experts and marriage partners Les and Leslie Parrott pose an important question in *The Time-Starved Marriage:* "What are you busy *doing*?" Think about it! Why is this so important? Because lack of time and attention kills intimacy in a marriage. No matter how committed a couple is, a subtle emptiness and a restless void camp out in every relationship when they don't make time for one another a priority.

Here are some ways to ease the time crunch:

- ♥ **Carve out a few minutes every evening** so you can reconnect. Train your children to understand that Mommy and Daddy need some time to talk without interruptions. When the children are very young, set the timer for them.

- ♥ **Consider eating a meal alone together** after the children have been served and are in bed. While you're waiting, serve a fancy tray of raw vegetables or cheese and crackers with sparkling cider.

- ♥ If you have teenagers who roam the house freely at odd hours, **reserve the family room with the fireplace** for the two of you from eight to ten one evening; explain to them that they must stay in their rooms.

- ♥ If you can swing it, let a college student stay with your children after the kids' bedtime in exchange for free laundry privileges. **Meet your husband at a coffee house** for hand holding and chatting.

- ♥ **Make a backyard date.** Play fort, set up a small tent, spend time on the porch swing, or check out the kids' trampoline.

- ♥ **Accompany your husband on that business trip** when he asks. Attend a presentation or an awards dinner.

> My husband once served as the executive director of the Children's Center (an organization combining law enforcement and medical, counseling, and social work teams for children who have been severely abused). Each year the center held a big fundraising and awareness event called the Valentine Gala. It was a very dressy affair and was vitally important for exposure in the community. During this event, my husband was responsible for, among other things, delivering a succinct, moving, and hard-hitting presentation about the center's work.
>
> One year the Gala unavoidably conflicted with my return from a speaking engagement in Phoenix, Arizona. The event began a half hour after my plane was to land. I was

worn out and wanted to go home, throw on my cozy robe, and cuddle with my little girls. But I knew my attendance at the Gala was important to Greg.

I drove home from the airport, kissed and squeezed the children, and let them pick out my jewelry and shoes while I rattled off instructions to the sitters. I put exactly four curls in my hair, freshened my makeup, and threw on my evening gown.

I made it to the Gala, a little stressed, but only ten minutes late. I knew it was worth it because, from the moment I walked in the door, staff and volunteers said things like: "We saw your plane landing," "Greg's been waiting for you," "Greg's in the dining room—he said to please find him first thing," and "Wow...you just got back, didn't you?" When I finally made it through the pre-dinner milling crowd to my husband, the smile that lit up his face made that small sacrifice very worth it.

♥ **Make your table the centerpiece of family life.** We live in a fast food culture. Let's not confuse that convenience with the possibility of having real fast relationships! Slow it down and exchange it for family meals that are prepared together and served by candlelight. My friend Sharris and her husband, David, are excellent cooks. Every time I enjoy a meal there, I am stunned at how much difference the presentation makes. They enjoy cooking together and their teamwork is the culinary equivalent of *Dancing with the Stars.*

♥ **Cut back driving time** whenever possible. For every ten minutes spent in an automobile, you reduce the time for relationships by ten-percent![2] We act like minivans were created on the eighth day so that now we can eat in them as God intended.

♥ **Redeem the time!** When our schedules are out of whack it results in a work imbalance, a relationship imbalance, and a sleep imbalance. That costs us in terms of health, focus, energy, and joy. Randy Frazee, author of *Making Room for Life,* has outlined a plan based on the Hebrew day that is not dissimilar to the lives of the early pioneers. Work hard during the daylight hours Monday through Saturday, but make room for play, rest, and relaxation at the end of each of those days—all day on Sunday. It makes for thought-provoking reading.

♥ **Plan a "no plans" night.** What is it about us that makes us fill all available time with something?

♥ **Set your priorities.** Really. Are you really living the life you want to live? Or are you settling for the imitation of life that your peers say you need? What is it that matters most to you?

What steals our time?

Overwork. Experts say that even the "most gifted of us only get a total of four hours of effective work done in any given day."[3] Everything needs rest. Call it whatever you want: downtime, vacation, boundaries, margin. It all adds up to the same thing—rest. God rested on the seventh day when His work was done (Genesis 2:2-3). During the year of jubilee, God's people could rest from their debt (Leviticus 25:10). Do I hear an amen? As I love to point out, even dirt needs rest! It's called letting the land lie fallow (Exodus 23:11). And you know what? The rest ends up enriching the soil. Hmm...wonder if there could be any parallels.

Overcommitment. There's an unavoidable principle at work in our lives: Saying "yes" to one thing almost always means saying "no" to something else. Oh, you might not mean for it to, but it has that effect. You react a bit more grumpily, lose some sleep, take things more personally, and make everyone around you edgy. Crack go the eggshells, pop goes the weasel, crunch go the relationships.

Make a commitment to not accept any obligation without consulting your spouse. A good corollary to that is to not volunteer each other's time! As I am writing this very page, I am waiting for my husband to call me. I deliberately did not schedule any speaking engagements for these last two months because of my writing deadlines.

When one of my favorite churches in the entire world called to ask us to do a last-minute Valentine banquet, I knew I was free, but I didn't know Greg's schedule. Instead of instantly volunteering us, I said I would have an answer just as soon as I could speak with Greg. Similarly, when he gets a call asking if I will sing and sign the National Anthem at the annual Law Enforcement banquet, he says, "I'm not sure of her schedule. You'll need to ask her." We try to watch out for each other.

Taking each other for granted. "I'm going to drive down to the corner and call you!" I half seriously threatened my husband one evening. Our phone rang incessantly. When my husband answered these calls, he was often asked, "What are you doing?" He had an endearing, annoying, and thoughtful (to others) habit of telling the person on the other end of the line, "Oh, nothing much." And he says this no matter what is going on! It's a good thing they get him or I'd answer them, "Talking to you on the phone!"

He's getting better about it though. The other night, I heard him tell someone who wanted something from him immediately that he couldn't do it. He had promised me that he would hang around the house that night because he had to teach the following night. Good for him! And, good for us.

Giving in to the tyranny of the urgent. I grew up as a PK (preacher's kid), which essentially meant that I lived part of my life in parsonages and half of it wearing hand-me-downs. It also meant that my daddy had a 24/7 job. But guess what? I wasn't at all the stereotypical PK, and I know exactly why I wasn't. My dad refused to be governed by the "urgent."

I honestly cannot remember a single time that I needed my dad and he wasn't there. He and mom marvelously managed their schedules so that we never felt neglected, and we witnessed them having dates and special times together as well. In fact, my sister and I laugh at how we thought Happy Meals and Mexican TV dinners (our fare on their date nights) were treats! We never realized that they were out eating gourmet! Their model gave us such a lovely sense of security that we unconsciously sought similar relationships when the time came for us to consider marriage.

～

Does your spouse get the full meal deal complete with appetizers? Or are you just serving up the leftovers of your time? Do you break bread together, or just stab it, wolf it down, and hurry on to the next thing?

I love what John Wesley said: "I never undertake any more work than I can go through with perfect calmness of spirit." Mr. Wesley was a busy, busy man (aren't we all?), but he was wise enough to choose his work and select carefully how he spent his time.

The Bitter End of the Excuse

Are you an excuse maker? In other words, do you constantly tell your spouse, your children, and your friends, "I know I'm grumpy right now, but I'm just…a little short on sleep…behind at work…frustrated with some things that are going on." You fill in the blank with your favorite excuse. I've been guilty of that, and I'm aware that after a while the excuse wears thin. There will always be something.

Stephen Covey got it right when he so deftly nailed our excuses. "The challenge is not to manage time, but to manage ourselves." I know, I know. We've all heard it. You have the same number of hours in your day that was given to Albert Einstein, Mother Teresa, Martin Luther King, and every president we've ever had. The only reason we don't like that point is because it's a good one. We all mysteriously make time for the crying infant who has to nurse or be rocked; for the toddler who's on the big girl potty chair yelling, "Come wipe me!" We make time to grocery shop and pay bills. We scrapbook or jog or shop. How can it possibly be any less important to make time for our spouse.

"In a national survey of married couples, researchers found that, on average, we spend less than three minutes of meaningful conversation together in a typical day."[4] To increase those minutes, for both of you it's going to mean turning off the TV, shutting the book, or getting off the phone.

To include our husbands in our decisions and to solicit their advice and opinion is to *value* them. It shows that we respect their judgment, trust their good will toward us, and acknowledge their insights. It's a sweet way to do life together.

Doing life together is vastly underrated. It's sweet. It's mundane. It's a dizzying, delicious batter of victories, heartaches, and heartbreaks. It's sharing successes and slogging through sorrows. Just tonight, I sat typing out notes for this book, listening to the sweet chatter of my four children and the rugged voice of my husband doing one of his best things (other than crime scene investigations)—being a daddy. They were learning to play a new card game and laughing in the next room. They were doing it so I could have the best of both worlds: I could meet my writing deadline and still feel included in family life.

During the game, Greg slipped away for a few moments to check a quote I wanted his opinion on. He put his arm around my shoulder and said proudly, "Sometimes, I still can't believe that you write books!" It was a simple gesture, but it rang loudly with his support.

Abraham Lincoln was reportedly sitting in the newspaper office of the *State Journal* in Springfield, Illinois when the news came to him from the telegraph office across the street that he had been nominated for president by the Republican party at its Chicago convention. "Mr. Lincoln, you are nominated on the third ballot," the telegraph operator wrote on a scrap of paper.

"Lincoln stared at the piece of paper silently amid the tumultuous shouts and cheers of his friends all around him. Then he rose, tucked the piece of paper into his pocket, and said quietly, 'There's a little woman down at our house who would like to hear this. I'll go down and tell her.'"[5]

Make it a practice to share your joys and success with your spouse first. While you're at it, help him succeed too. Gary Chapman suggests three simple questions to help your spouse succeed. Ask:

1. What can I do to help you?

2. How can I make your life easier?

3. How can I be a better wife (husband)?[6]

Listen carefully to the answers and prepare to hear your name in your husband's future success stories. It's true—behind every great man there really is a great woman!

Home Weather Conditions

Suppose your local morning news weather forecaster came to your home. What would he or she predict about today's climate and conditions at your house?

- ♥ Gloomy with a chance of heavy moping in the late afternoon.

- ♥ Major fit throwing forecast because husband is unlikely to remember to call home via wife's unspoken expectation (see Rule #11 in the marriage playbook).

- ♥ Storm clouds brewing after a severe case of cabin fever struck, stranding the wife alone with copious amounts of little people.

- ♥ Weepy with a chance of heavy showers later on unless a surprise Starbucks run or box of red light Krispy Kreme donuts arrives for the wife with no expectation of having to share.

- ♥ Sunny with periodic bursts of pleasantness and sprinkles of sweetness.

- ♥ General goodwill conditions likely to thrive in atmosphere where warm fronts of tenderness and affection continue to run along the house's southern exposure windows.

If we don't watch our home weather conditions, storms threaten and the stability of relationships can deteriorate quickly. In her book

A House Full of Friends, Susan Alexander Yates identifies three traps in marital friendship.[7]

The picky trap occurs when we realize that no matter what our spouse does to fulfill our needs or meet our expectations, it wouldn't be enough. We would just find something else about which to gripe, complain, or nag. Think this couldn't be you? Have you ever requested that your husband help you with a specific task or do something around the house only to trail behind him offering your suggestions on how to make it better? Or follow him, commenting about what he's doing wrong? Our husbands can rightfully view us as impossible to please and it thwarts their desire to be helpful.

One time I asked Greg why he didn't help with kitchen clean-up as often as he used to. "Do you really want to know?" he asked. That should have been my clue. "It doesn't seem like you really want me to because you make clucking noises about water going on the floor, offer a running commentary about the best way to load the dishwasher, and you do that hissing thing if I drop crumbs while I'm wiping the counters."

The comparison trap can sneak up on us. Truthfully, most of us are pretty content with our lives, our homes, our bodies, and our children until we begin to compare them with someone else's. We watch television and become dissatisfied with our incomes and our romances. A new magazine arrives in the mail and suddenly we simply cannot stand our ugly couch and the boring color of our family room. Our child that plugs away diligently and makes Bs is doing a terrific job until we meet Janet Jump-Up at parent-teacher conferences. She accosts us with a list of her child's activities and accomplishments hardly pausing for breath. Then our child is in danger of being nagged to death to keep up. Advertisements berate us for not having thin enough waistlines, white enough teeth, up-to-date enough clothing, and then poke fun at the pathetically lame cars we have to drive.

If you are tumbling down this trap, turn off the TV and unsubscribe to that magazine for a while. Tape up lists around the house of all you have to be thankful for.

We have friends that make more than double our income. They are miserable because they're not only keeping up with those mysterious Jones's, they're trying to change their last name to Jones! When I start to envy, I try to remember that it seems like for lots of people expenses rise to meet available income.

We know a family whose 14-year-old daughter was just diagnosed with leukemia. We pray for them and our hearts break. It renews our commitment to be grateful; not to take for granted the health of our children.

I meet women who are throwing away happiness with both hands—battling anorexia, trying to hide an affair, or spending every spare minute at the gym for fear their husband might meet someone younger. What an exhausting way to live. For all of us. It might be simpler just to turn our eyes from what we don't have to what we do.

Last, there's **the hopeless trap**. This is the most deadly trap. It leads to a marriage of disillusionment and misery. If you're determined to believe that nothing in your marriage will ever change, you're probably right. But as long as you have hope, and work to be an agent of change in *yourself,* nothing is impossible because nothing is impossible for God! The bright gift of hope, of belief in your marriage, is a treasure.

Roll over and greet your mate with a gentle kiss or a quick back rub. Kiss like lovers before you part for the day. Whisper a sweet message or spend a few seconds just holding each other tightly.

Statistically, homecomings are among the most significant times in a marriage. When you have been apart during the day, it is the first seven seconds after you reunite that set the tone for the entire evening! Make them a good seven seconds.

Relax together every evening, even if it's just for ten minutes. Shower together. Read together. Pray together.

Don't neglect the nonsexual part of your marriage's intimacy health either. It's easy to neglect, criticize, belittle, withdraw, and disapprove. It's challenging to deliberately nurture, build up, get involved, and praise.

Don't force your spouse to participate in a sport, or activity, or attend the ballet with you if he absolutely hates it. It won't be fun and you'll both be miserable unless it's entered into willingly.

Cultivating Spiritual Life Together

If you and your spouse are believers, it is so important that you have a consistent prayer life together. Consider reading through a daily devotional together and praying at the end of those times. Pick up a copy of the *Couples' Devotional Bible*. After one reads the Scripture, the other can read the devotion. Perhaps you could commit to following one of the many programs that lead you through reading the Bible in one year—read individually, then together share insights, ask questions, and pray afterwards.

Perhaps one of you is more of a planner. You could adapt this plan for a daily ten-minute prayer time:

> **Five minutes**—Scripture reading. Choose a scripture that is especially meaningful to you or that addresses a situation which you are currently experiencing.
>
> **Two minutes**—One prays.
>
> **Two minutes**—The other prays.
>
> **One minute**—Be silent before the Lord.
>
> **Monday, Wednesday, Friday**—Husband takes the lead.
>
> **Tuesday, Thursday, Saturday**—Wife takes the lead.
>
> **Sunday**—The Lord leads.[8]

At a weekly connection meeting, make a point of asking your spouse how you can specifically pray for him during the coming week. Really share with each other. This is challenging, but work at making it a priority; the results will be worth it. Pray this way for your children too. Let them see you praying with and for your husband, as well as with and for them.

If your spouse is not a believer, hold firm. First Peter 3:1-2 urges,

"Wives, in the same way be submissive to your husbands so that, if any of them do not believe the word, they may be won over without words by the behavior of their wives, when they see the purity and reverence of your lives."

Sharing the Gift of Chocolate

Enjoy the wonder of true chocolate with your spouse. These make the perfect romantic getaway treats, ideal for snacking on during a road trip or feeding one another once you arrive...even if your destination is merely your bedroom.

Romantic M&M's Bars

½ cup butter

2 eggs

2 tsp. vanilla

¾ cup sugar

¾ cup brown sugar

1 tsp. baking powder

1½ cups flour

½ tsp. salt

1 cup vanilla chips

1 cup M&M's

⅓ cup miniature chocolate kisses

Cream liquid ingredients; add mixed dry ingredients. Stir in chips and M&M's Spoon into greased 9x13 inch pan and spread evenly. Sprinkle top with kisses. Bake at 350 degrees for 20-25 minutes. Cool on wire rack, cut into bars. If you're home, serve warm with a dollop of vanilla ice cream.

The Little Glitches

We sat around the tables of the Pizza Hut Express in Target on a chilly February night celebrating that all the children met their school reading goals. They were happy eating their coupon purchased, personal pan pizzas, leaving Greg and me sort of free to talk.

"By the way," my husband mentioned casually. "I've been asked to teach the night police academy on the fourteenth."

"The fourteenth that is Valentine's Day? That fourteenth?" My voiced squeaked. "Does the academy even *have* class that day?"

"Yup. The coordinator said he would understand if I couldn't; I can make up that section another night."

I was still stuck on the fact that the academy didn't suspend all instruction on the day of love. "No wonder most cops have such lousy marriages," I muttered under my breath. Well, never let it be said that I can't rise to the occasion. We didn't have any extra money anyway, and I suspected that my sweetheart had not yet made any grand plans. "Go for it!" I told him.

He eyed me suspiciously and I plotted away. I'd already gotten him a red lantern in anticipation of a small bedroom redo (just a new comforter set and some paint) later this summer and a sorely needed new bathrobe. I'd thrown in a pair of boxers and some ornery lover's dice for good measure. Now I knew just what to do with them. I'd make a trail of chocolate kisses leading up to his classroom (much better than the usual trails of blood he has to follow in his line of work) and lay the items on his desk, wrapping the two more personal items. Each small gift would be accompanied by a clue, asking him to imagine how we could celebrate our love when he arrived home!

I could be waiting for him after class for a quick rendezvous at Starbucks, flirt with him outrageously all the way there and all the way home, and then—well, anything could happen!

I'll let you know how that went sometime!

A lot of what determines whether we view a situation as a tragedy or a comedy in the making depends on our outlook. "Life is," my mother often admonished us, "mostly what you make it." I think

I'll go for an epic adventure film with comedic moments and lots of romance thrown in.

Checklist:

Look for love in all the right places. Be sure to notice the little things your husband does for you that might not seem romantic in the traditional or Hollywood sense of the word, but are truly expressions of his love for you.

- ♥ Mowing the lawn
- ♥ Watching over the children when he can see you've had it
- ♥ Remembering what your favorite soda or tea is when you dine out
- ♥ Surrendering his desire to see an action movie in favor of the chick flick he knows you'd rather see
- ♥ Letting you eat the buttered layer of the popcorn first
- ♥ Taking a quick shower when he knows you want to wash your hair
- ♥ Navigating the MapQuest site for you when you're taking a trip by yourself
- ♥ Encouraging you to enjoy time with your friends
- ♥ Listening to your mother talk about her to-do list and her physical ailments
- ♥ Holding you when you cry
- ♥ Killing the creepy crawlies that occasionally invade the home
- ♥ Making the Saturday morning pancakes
- ♥ Letting you sleep in
- ♥ Bringing you the baby so you don't have to get out of bed yet again
- ♥ Gassing up the car and arranging the luggage "just so" before you go on vacation
- ♥ The tender way he roughhouses with the kids on the floor
- ♥ The sexy way he winks at you across the room

CHOCOLATE-COVERED QUESTIONS

1. List five new interests or hobbies that you'd be willing to check out together. Rank your favorites.

   a.

   b.

   c.

   d.

   e.

2. How has marriage made you a better person? Be specific.

3. Do men have the "harlequin-wrapped world" equivalent of romantic expectations for marriage?

4. What prevents us from appreciating the nontraditional gestures of romance?

5. How did you score on the marital drift quiz? Were you surprised or alarmed by this? What immediate things can you change to protect your relationship?

6. Which time stealers (overwork, overcommitment, taking each other for granted, the tyranny of the urgent) are the most pervasive in your marriage? Which of them would be the easiest to get under control? Make a concrete plan for taking back your time together.

SCRIPTURE

*"If it is possible, as far as it depends on you,
live at peace with everyone" (Romans 12:18).*

HOT CHOCOLATE TOPIC

Do you feel like we're taking each other for granted? How
could I best show you that I love doing life with you?

GOODNIGHT KISS

Honey, if I've forgotten to thank you for all the little things you do for me, I want to do it now. Thanks for being such a good provider, lover, and student of so many things that I like best.

HOW DO YOU DECIDE WHO TO MARRY?

You got to find somebody who likes the same stuff.
Like, if you like sports, she should like it that you like sports,
and she should keep the chips and dip coming.

ALAN, AGE 10

Chocolate Drops
When Children Come Along

*The husband encouraged his wife: "Remember, dear,
the hand that rocks the cradle rules the world."
She handed him a diaper and said, "Well, take over the world
for three hours while I go get my hair done."*

STORY FOUND IN MY DADDY'S SERMON NOTES

Who'd have ever thought the love of your life would be short, chunky, and bald? Having a baby changes everything! This is a paraphrase of a Johnson's baby product ad. And it's true. For most of us the transfer of affections begins the moment the stick in our hands has two lines in the little window (or the moment we officially call the attorney and begin adoption proceedings), and it ends the first time we hold them in our arms. Having a child is the only instance in which I can be certain that love at first sight exists!

But oh, how children change the landscape of marriage! Is it the first night that one of you pretends to sleep so the other one has to get up with the baby? Does it happen when sleep is chosen over sexual intimacy more times than you'd care to admit? How about when conversations come down to the color of baby's bodily emissions or the quest for identifying various substances on mom's shoulder? Is it—yikes!—when husband and wife begin calling each other mom and dad? Children sweeten the atmosphere, disrupt the spontaneity, and sour the schedules.

Children arrive as pint-size dictators, wreaking a coup with an army of one. From the moment I held each of them in my arms, they commandeered my heart, my mind, my thoughts, ninety percent of my brain cells, and yes, even my breasts. I had once boasted that children would not change my life much; they were small and they would just have to adjust to my schedule as I schlepped them along in cute, matching baby slings. Ha.

Schedule, schmedule! Sleep becomes the most precious commodity in the house when you have one or more small children. Lack of it causes you to morph into a hateful, baggy-eyed version of your former self. During this stage my husband once took a nap without asking my permission and I wouldn't wash his boxers for a week. I zealously monitored which of us got more sleep and made vicious threats to the electric nursery monitor whenever all its lights lit up like an air traffic control tower.

Given all this, I was baffled by the fact that my husband actually drew a smiley face on his calendar on the date of my six-week checkup. For a time, sex seemed incongruous with motherhood. How could my husband possibly be attracted to someone with leaking breasts, a stomach the consistency of Jell-O, and mood swings that rivaled turnovers in a pro basketball game? Likewise, on my last night of nursing each of the girls, I always crept back to our room in tears. As much as he wanted to be sympathetic, his gut level response was, "Yes! They're mine again!"

I felt exhausted, frumpy, and pulled apart in a thousand directions. No matter how I tried, I couldn't turn that insidious kind of tired known as "mommy tired" into an aphrodisiac. Given the choice between sex and sleep, I, like many moms, chose (or wanted to choose) sleep every time.

I could no longer recall normal. It made me feel ever so much better when someone mercifully voiced what I was thinking: Normal is just a setting on the washing machine.

Another unknown wit said, "There are three ways to get something done: do it yourself, hire someone, or forbid your kids to do it." This, in a nutshell, is the adventure of raising children. You know this to be true when you find yourself giggling in a corner after threatening your child with swats if he doesn't stay in bed. It's the child's response that sends you over the edge—in serious, contemplative preschool mode he inquires, "How many?" in order to size up whether or not disobeying is worth it.

Labor and Longings

No more staying awake for two movie rentals on the weekend, one chick flick and one action movie. Indeed, Greg and I have a list of movies that we'd like to know the endings to; we plan to re-rent them somewhere between the girls' college years and the nursing home. Gone are late night discussions of the Brownings, C.S. Lewis, the latest John Grisham novel, or even the O'Reilly Factor, for heaven's sake! Instead, you find yourself swapping cute kid stories and going on double dates just so you can trade labor and delivery tales and toddler antics with other people who understand that you're utterly consumed with this parenthood thing.

My friend Susie wins the best "my water broke story." She and her husband were expecting their first child and had just purchased a water bed. Susie's side of the bed was too close to the wall to get out easily, so she crawled across her husband, Scott, to use the bathroom. While she was straddling him, getting ready to swing her other leg over the side of the bed, it happened. She was confused (had she broken the bed?) and then embarrassed. "Gosh, Scott, I'm sorry. I think I just peed on you!"

We got top honors for labor horror stories (they seem to be endless, ranging from 32 hour labors to the ten minute "precipitous labor" resulting in no drugs for me and consequently no feeling remaining in the fingers of my husband's left hand). Those stories include the one about the birthing center nurse who was going to purchase our home from us; she entered the room during a contraction with a newspaper ad circled in purple marker. She wanted to know whether or not my husband would hire that particular contractor to cut down the mulberry tree in our soon-to-be-ex-front yard!

After sleep, the next biggest longing is probably for adult conversation. It seems harder to come by with each successive child. One couple told me that what they missed the most about their three children growing older was the private conversations they'd once enjoyed on long car trips while the kids either napped soundly in car seats or were so young they were oblivious to the topic. "Now they're miniature eavesdroppers and they repeat everything! Not only is there no chance of talking uninterrupted, but we have such a limited range of subjects it doesn't seem like we ever have the chance to talk about what's really important." Ugh. There's nothing like the feeling that our own children are tattling on us.

I've experienced this firsthand more than once. Our youngest daughter's Sunday school teacher pulled us aside to share a story. Apparently the preschool class had been talking about how God provides us with everything we need..."Kind of like your parents do!" Miss Linda enthused. Elexa raised her hand and with four-year-old drama announced, "Not my parents. We're on a budget!"

I'd like to say a special word to moms who have chosen to base their careers at home for a season. We are especially prone to loneliness, isolation, and placing too much of the communication and "rescue me" burden on our husbands.

Despite the privilege, and it *is* a privilege, of staying home with our children and being CEO of home management, it is still easy to take issue with our hardworking husbands when they say that they are showing love by working to provide for the family. He'd have to go to work and earn money even if he weren't married. Yes, but consider this, he wouldn't be doing it "with the same commitment, intent, sacrifice, and depth of passion that he has when he's doing it for his woman and his children."[1]

I don't always succeed, but I've been making a concerted effort to change my attitude, at least in front of our girls. "I know Daddy's late...has been gone a lot this semester...hasn't called yet (or whatever the situation), but I am so proud of your daddy. He is very good at what he does and I am thankful that he works hard so that I get to spend most of my time home with you guys." That usually brings little smiles all around. And oh, the squeals when the garage door starts opening, "Daddy's home!" My husband is truly one of the hardest working individuals I know, but he has time for everybody.

I am blessed to have a husband who will squeeze me tightly after I have been away for a night speaking and say, "Honey, you have a hard job! I couldn't do this all the time." He has also told me how much easier it is for him to know that he doesn't have to worry about who is with the children or what happens when the unexpected glitch comes up, because I am usually there to take care of it.

That said, I have interests and concerns about various minutiae, which no matter how much my sweetheart cares about *me,* he doesn't care to hear about in detail. Enter the girlfriends! They will care about how neat the centerpieces and take-home favors were at the last retreat where I spoke. They will agonize with me about whether or not I was too sharp with my eight-year-old during a grumpy moment. They'll tell me that the blue pumps with that suit look ridiculous. And yes, they'll even tell me if those khaki shorts make my rear look big!

In other words, girlfriends are a necessity for all of us, but especially when we feel like the Lone Ranger trapped on a secluded ranch with Robin Hood and his band of merry, or not-so-merry-before-naptime, munchkins all day.

Go over to each other's homes to visit and exchange cleaning day parties. Meet for lunch at the park. Form a book club or discussion group. Join MOPS (Mothers of Preschoolers), Moms in Touch, or Bible Study Fellowship. Create a network of mentors as well as peers who are going through the same stages and frustrations of motherhood. Just the realization that you're not as alone as you thought you were is a huge help. A mutual cry into vanilla lattes and fat-free hot chocolates piled high with whipped cream doesn't hurt either.

And since kids generally cause your thoughts to bounce around randomly from subject to subject (you'll probably notice that this chapter is written a bit differently than all the others; unless of course *you* have children and then you'll think it all makes perfect sense!) here's a scary thought: Your children will learn the art of being married by watching you! They will turn into cabinet slammers, conflict avoiders, passive doormats, or passionate, positive mates someday—make the model they see a godly one.

Marriage First

When the Bible talks about generational sin, it doesn't mean that God forces us to repeat the sins of our parents. Rather, it acknowledges that many of us *do*. Be the first to break the cycle by learning about and then practicing healthy relationship skills.

Jill Savage, founder and president of Hearts at Home, a wonderful organization dedicated to encouraging moms and professionalizing motherhood, often tells moms to ask themselves this question: Is yours a child-centered family or a marriage-centered family? The answer usually makes most of us squirm. So, we know what it is that we need to do, but where do we start?

"Start by identifying a major misconception: 'I could never leave my children, they need me. Besides, no one can care for their needs as well as I can.'

"I believed that...I believed that leaving them occasionally would rob them of a stable environment. I believed that no one, not even their dad, could care for their needs as I could.

"And my marriage was falling apart in the midst of it all."[2]

~

I'd like to share a column that I wrote on our decade anniversary. It illustrates perfectly the tug a mother feels when she knows that her marriage deserves to come first, but her heart urges her to stay with the children.

Either my husband or I will be with our children approximately 359 days this year. It is the other six days which consume me with guilt.

In celebration of a decade of marriage and the four children for whom we will tenderly care during the remainder of the year, we are selfishly going on a cruise for six blissfully child-free days. The income tax refund check arrives and with it I pay the cruise fee, five months in advance. It's a pittance compared with what we've spent on school supplies, shoes, clothing, braces, toothpaste, apple juice, animal crackers, underwear, training wheels, training bras, two sports, and three kinds of lessons. But I'm smitten with guilt. Surely we could do something more practical, more urgent with this money.

Two weeks to go and I make final arrangements which sound, well final, with my mother who will watch over them while we are gone. Despite the fact that she and Daddy raised my sister and me reasonably well and with no missing parts, I leave her five pages of typewritten instructions. Bedtimes. Who's allowed over to play. What they can have for snacks (I don't know why I bother with that one; Mimi always let's them have junk). What songs to sing to the three-year-old and what her favorite stories are. I even remind her to brush their teeth! At the bottom, my husband and I type our wishes for the girls if anything should happen to us. He signs his with a flourish; I sign mine reluctantly. The letters are smudged by one fat round teardrop. God, please let me return to my babies safely.

While packing, I am trailed by children who eye me somberly, occasionally make tackling motions around my knees, and who alternate between ignoring me completely or covering me in kisses. It doesn't matter. The cold shoulder and the overpowering affection both pierce me with remorse. *It will be good for you to get away and remember that you are somebody's wife.*

I fold one new, bright sundress, purchased especially for the trip, and wonder if I still remember how to do this—not to be a mother. I finger the lingerie from my bottom left-hand drawer, marveling at how little there is. Nervously I shove it into the suitcase as well. Makeup, curling irons, barrettes, and an array of vacationy smelling lotions (coconut, lime, peach, vanilla) tumble into a carry-on next to Greg's sparse collection of needs—deodorant, toothbrush, hairbrush. They mix in a zany visual reminder that we are one. God ordained it thus.

In the wee hours of the morning we depart. I am folding last minute loads of laundry. Sorting little socks. Plastering every drawer, cabinet, and refrigerator shelf with hectic sticky note messages of love, reassurance, and lipstick kisses. We tiptoe into each girl's room, lean over their beds, and press goodbye kisses to sweet, sleepy heads. I breathe short little prayers over them. Their eyes flutter slightly and they smile. As we leave, small noses press against an upstairs window and tiny hands wave. I only cry for the first two hours of the trip.

By day three, I remember. My mind shuffles back to another beach where younger, thinner versions of Greg and Cindy held hands, whispered, dreamed, planned, and discovered each other. I relax, allowing myself the unexpected gifts of room service, maid service, someone else to cook, to clean up. I take long walks with Greg and notice anew that I have married quite the man. He is tender, witty, romantic, and incredibly forgiving of my oh-so-noticeable efforts not to mention the children.

He ignores the way I show everyone in the airport shuttle their pictures. He pretends he doesn't see me stuffing unique napkins from a restaurant into my purse, knowing they will get a kick out of them when we return home. He indulges me when I beg for his input on whether to bring them back the pens with the floating ships or the Cruise Barbie for them to share.

He does this because sprinkled in between such times are moonlit strolls, uninterrupted conversations, playful intimacies, and the gradual return of the woman he fell in love with.

The last morning away I realize there have been lessons for everyone. Greg knows that I truly do value him most, more than anything on this earth. I have learned that cleaving to my husband is well worth the effort. We have given our children both a lesson and a gift—the security of parents who love each other enough to work at our marriage and the certainty that we will always come home.

Need further convincing? "Many sociological studies have confirmed it is more important to a child that mommy and daddy love each other than it is that mommy and daddy love the child."[3]

So what's the solution...other than farming the kids out every weekend? Now and then avoid the "Deadly Three Ds." If you let them, kids will:

1. **Dominate**. The schedule. The conversation. The entertainment. Basically, your life. Instead, show them (this will eventually turn into training) that your time together is valuable. Let them in on the action of getting you ready for a date night. Little ones love to be big helpers!

   Make sure that you give them the security of being heard and plenty of attention too. By far, the best time for this as a family is the dinner hour. Make it special. We have a flexible dinner event schedule that we adhere to on most weeks:

   Monday—book night. We break all etiquette rules and everyone is allowed to read at the table. We share plots, wonderful quotes or insights, and why we like what we're reading.

Tuesday and Thursday—table talk. Planned discussions using conversation starters or almost anything more specific than "How was your day?" (See pages 101-02 in *Who Got Peanut Butter on My Daily Planner?* for sample family conversation starters.)

Wednesday and Friday—family devotions. Simple Scripture readings (the chapter of Proverbs, which corresponds to the date of the month, works well) or a children's devotional can provide age appropriate chunks of God's Word on which to feed.

Saturday—free day. We might watch a movie together, talk about nothing, or stare into space.

Sunday—family night. This is a sacred tradition in our family and we all look forward to it. We watch old movies, home movies, or classic TV dramas and sitcoms (*Andy Griffith, The Waltons, Little House on the Prairie, The Cosby Show, Bewitched, The Brady Bunch, Dr. Quinn, Medicine Woman, The Doris Day Show*), have a short devotion, sing a few praise choruses, and close with family prayer time, lifting up praise, the needs around us, and specific trials or joys we will be facing during the coming week.

During the summertime, we step it up for nine weeks into Super Summer Family Night! They're a bit longer and sometimes include field trips. We always have fun object lesson devotions and a summer memory program. (I'd be happy to email you a sample list!) All six of us have a verse to memorize every week and receive a small prize as a reward. The catch is, the verses build on each other; in order to get the next week's prize, you have to know that week's verse and all the preceding verses! On the first night, each child gets a typed sheet with all the memory verses. Using highlighter, we mark shorter versions for the youngest children. Prizes have included Nerds ropes, a coupon for staying up fifteen minutes past bedtime, neon gel pens, ice cream cones, and dollar store notebooks which I personalized with scrapbook stickers. By the end of the program, all family members have nine memory verses hidden in their hearts. Working together on this common goal also functions as a great marriage builder.

2. **Divide and conquer.** Children seem to learn strategy and tactics at a young age. They discover that pitting one parent against the other can be effective. If you have more than one child, the older one will often send in the youngest, and presumably the cutest, to wield influence. Make sure you check with each other before issuing a verdict or giving permission. Once you've established this policy, the troops will retreat, at least until tomorrow.

3. **Devour your time.** I had the privilege of speaking at the Hearts at Home International Conference in Vienna, Austria with author and speaker, Kendra Smiley. She has an engaging and practical, philosophical talk and wonderful book all by the same name: *Be the Parent!* It's the best advice for the third D. If your children are running your household, then you have abdicated your God-given role as parent. Children aren't to run our lives—we're to train them to someday live their own!

Forming a Family Foundation

By the way we nurture our marriages, live our lives, and pass along godly wisdom and love, we build a family's foundation.

Go for planned spontaneity.

This is particularly necessary for sexual intimacy. As the kids get older and become more aware of the physical aspects of marriage, if you don't already have one, get a lock for your bedroom door. When they're gone for an overnight sleepover, anything goes. With a teenager in the house, things have gotten infinitely trickier. One evening a few months ago, Eden came in our room and found us sitting on the edge of the bed kissing. She rolled her eyes. "Gross you guys! Get a room!" I giggled about being caught by my own teen "making out" with her dad.

Greg grinned. "Guess what? This *is* our room!"

Eden's eyes widened as she backed out of the room. "Oh. Yeah."

You schedule everything else that's important to you: income tax filing, your annual pap smear, the piano recital, and the basketball tournament. So add sex, date nights, and annual retreats to your fun side list of "must dos." A common survey complaint under the question, "What factors inhibit physical intimacy in your marriage?" was a single word: children. As someone once said, "Sex makes little kids; kids make little sex." Make sure this isn't true of your marriage.

Be honest and open.

Make sure that facts about marriage and intimacy come from you. Encourage daddy-daughter dates. They will learn to expect wonderful treatment and have high standards for their own dates someday. They will also learn a healthy appreciation for sex and its unique role to marriage if they get truthful, solid information from you.

I've always explained to my girls whatever information they requested, but didn't elaborate until two separate talks. I initiated the first one when they were around seven years old. We talked about basic plumbing differences and used correct anatomical terms in a matter-of-fact tone. I didn't yet use the term sex, but instead referred to a special way of loving that God designed only for mommies and daddies. I explained that yes, sometimes people can choose not to follow God's plan and have a baby outside of marriage, but that way isn't best for anyone. We also talked in general terms about the changes they could expect while enjoying the process of becoming young ladies. Make talking about purity and modesty for both boys and girls part of your usual interaction. Be sure and model the qualities you want to see in your child; ask them if they have any questions.

Around age ten, I took them somewhere special and went into a bit more depth. We talked about menstruation, shaving legs, and using deodorant. I brought a pad, panty liner, and tampon with me and let them open them and ask questions. Some of the questions were insightful and thoughtful; some of them made me smile. I'm not an authority because I haven't had the privilege of seeing the story of how my girls turned out. But it tells me something that my oldest daughter saved those things in her special box, and my second daughter squeezed me and told me that our night talk in a gazebo under the stars would be one of her favorite memories. Two down, two to go! Whew!

I am planning to do an overnight retreat with each girl between ages 12 and 13 in order to go into more detail about purity and dating. My hope is to combine celebration and fun times with godly instruction.

Let go of resentment.

Flip Wilson once said, "If I had my entire life to live over, I doubt if I'd have the strength!" Most of us who are wives and mothers would second that statement with a rousing chorus of "amens"! We're tired, cranky, pressured, and yes, resentful.

Instead of appreciating what both parents bring to the household, we play games. "I do more around here than you." "I'm the biggest income contributor." "I'm with the children more than you ever thought about being." You know the drill.

When Greg and I travel, the scenario is worlds apart. For one thing, he doesn't usually travel that much, but when he does he's usually gone for a week at a time. He comes home from work, asks me to get out my calendar, and announces the dates he'll be gone.

I usually speak two times a month, except in the summer, and am gone one or two nights each time. But in contrast, I give him my schedule twelve months in advance, grocery shop and put a list of menu options on the refrigerator, compile a list of the kids' activities, and lay out the younger one's clothes along with notes about who has to have tennis shoes on what days. He's not incompetent by any means, but I am the mother, which means I suffer enormous guilt every time I have to leave, plus (to quote Junie B. Jones) I have their schedules down to a science.

If we're not careful, the contrast can be a source of conflict instead of complement. Model this simple Triple A list for resolving challenges and teach it to your children.

> **Affirmation:** You can respect someone and behave respectfully toward them even if you disagree with their viewpoint or behavior.
>
> **Assertion:** Describe the behavior or situation which is causing you frustration and indicate your feelings about it without attacking personhood or character.
>
> **Action:** Clearly identify a reasonable way in which you would like to see the other person's behavior change.[4] For example, "Honey, I really appreciate you helping me get the kids ready for bed. I'm just really frustrated when they read past the agreed upon lights out. It would really help me if you would help enforce this so they're not cranky when I wake them up for school in the morning." Respectful, direct communication is a great thing for kids to see when you're working out your differences and will equip them to deal with difficult people and situations as they grow.

Let good enough be okay.

Ask a lot of husbands why they don't help out more, and they'll tell you it's because their wives are always second-guessing them. They don't ever feel like the job is done to their wives' standards. Admittedly, sometimes we go on helicopter mode, sighing and making suggestions. We stand over them offering advice and corrections. Hover-ers of the world unite! And then dissipate! We need a support group. *It will be okay if I relinquish control.* Deep breath. *It will be okay if I relinquish control.*

If your husband doesn't diaper the baby the way you would...if the dishes get done, but not necessarily according to your pattern...if he rolls the towels instead of folding them, we've got to get over it! In the middle of certain parenting seasons, a lick and a promise when it comes to housecleaning is okay. As the children grow, make sure that you let them help you and give them their own little chores too.

Elisa Morgan and Carol Kuykendall put it this way: Children can complicate, deepen, and test commitment.[5] They can even adversely affect the way we deal with our mates. Remember that your husband is a man. It's painfully easy to begin treating him like another one of the children. "Love makes requests, not demands. When I demand things from my spouse, I become a parent and (he) the child."[6] In marriage, we are adult partners and the unequal footing of parent-child relationship has no place there. We constantly need reminding that we are on the same team. We may play different positions, but in the end, whatever contributions we're making add up to a winning game.

> *"The smile of a child is a tattoo: indelible art."*
> JODI PICOULT IN *MY SISTER'S KEEPER*

We recently had one of those inevitable teen discussions about quitting an activity with which our oldest had become bored. Greg was trying to reason with Eden about the benefits of "sticktoitiveness."

"But Dad, I don't see how doing something I don't want to do is going to help me later!"

I don't know what his response was because I beat a hasty retreat to our bedroom and stuffed the pillow in my mouth to keep from laughing. And then I really thought about that. What would happen if I only did what I felt like doing today?

I push snooze on the alarm button, burrow back into the down-filled mattress topper, and pull the fluffy comforter up to my chin. Sighing happily, a brief thought about how cold, dreary, and windy it is crosses the few brain cells that are conscious.

Half an hour later, the two oldest girls storm into my room wailing, "Mo-om! We overslept! How come you didn't wake us up? We're gonna be late for school!" Shrugging my shoulders, I stay where I am and wonder if child number three will wake up, and then I prepare to welcome child number four under my covers for a snuggle.

I hear them downstairs helping themselves to last night's chocolate cake, chocolate milk, and pretzels for breakfast. Oh, well. When they appear to be ready for school, I throw my terry-cloth robe on over my jeans and jammie shirt, climb into the minivan, and head over to the first of their schools. I kiss them each goodbye with sleepy wishes for a good day; I don't feel like walking them in today.

Since I'm already out and about, I pull on my sunglasses so Starbucks won't think I'm a victim of violent crime without my makeup and make the drive into town. Disregarding the budget (and my diet), I go for broke and order a venti hot chocolate with extra whipped cream and two blueberry muffins. What the heck. I woke up starved.

Back home, I build a fire and curl up with a shiny new magazine and a book I've been dying to read. I read for three hours straight, taking a break for a lunch of oyster crackers, a Krispy Kreme, and a Diet Coke with lime. Back to the couch and my book.

The phone rings twelve times between 8:00 a.m. and noon; I don't answer it once, vaguely hearing (and ignoring) the message machine pleas. Eden forgot her gym shoes, Emmy her library book. Ellie wants to know if she can have treat money, and Elexa would like me to bring Kindergarten bear to the school before nap time.

I pick up all the girls when school ends only because I don't want the office to call Greg. I let them fend for themselves for homework and after school snacks and allow the baby to watch a Max and Ruby video four times in a row.

Greg comes home with a big hug for me and a puzzled look. "What are you thinking for dinner tonight, hon?"

"Actually, I'm not thinking about it at all. Whatever you guys get."

They order in pizza. Seeing that I'm not really doing anything, Greg gets all the girls bathed, brushes their teeth, and parades them past me for goodnight kisses. Ignoring the general state of chaos, the sea of Legos and naked, headless Barbies and their accessories, he sits on the arm of the couch and gives me "the look."

I stare into his eyes and contemplate whether or not this is something I feel like doing tonight. After all, it would mean actually getting up and taking a shower...

You may laugh at the above silly daydream, but aside from the fact that motherhood, household management, marriage, and life in general are all just plain old hard, sometimes we're not too far from the "I just don't feel like it" thinking when it comes to balancing the equation of being a wife and being somebody's mother.

These days are precious and fleeting. This season of influence, memories, and irreplaceable treasure with your children will be gone before you know it. Laugh at life. Love them every chance you get. Listen to their hearts. Trust God with the little ones He loves even more than you do.

The Most Important Ingredient

If I spend my days building skyscraping block towers, assembling really cool stuff out of Legos, speaking gently to my children, building relationships with other moms over yummy and expensive drinks at

Starbucks, but have not love, I am only the siren button from the kids' ride-on fire truck, permanently and annoyingly stuck on hold.

If I have the gift of knowing exactly which child attempted to flush the Hot Wheels down the toilet, which one pushed her sister, which one is hiding a salamander in the closet, and of pointing out my husband's faults in excruciating detail (while failing to acknowledge any of my own); if I can fathom the mysteries of the BRAT diet, and the art of signing permission slips, icing the cupcakes, and starting the washer while nursing the baby; if I can balance the PTA budget, organize the book fair, and choose intimacy with my husband instead of sleep at least three nights a week (as per Dr. Kevin Leman); if I have faith that somehow we'll find both the lost car keys and the patience to tolerate an extended visit by the in-laws, but have not love, I am nothing.

If I save all my box tops and soup labels for the school drive, give outgrown clothing to the local shelter, send care packages to missionaries, and cook (from scratch!) for my husband and family most nights each week; if I surrender my body to the perils of childbirth, stretch marks, nursing, and dark under eye circles from too many sleepless nights, all without benefit of Botox, fake tanning, or diet bars; if I am the model of marital surrender from 1 Corinthians 7, but speak sarcastically to my husband, undermine his authority, or treat him disrespectfully because I have not love, I gain nothing—especially not romance, tenderness, or a solid mutual partnership, the way God intended.

Love is patient when someone isn't ready to use the big girl potty. It is kind when my husband has a hard day. It doesn't envy someone something which we can't afford on our salary, it does not boast about an unexpected idyll or superlative vacation. It is not proud, recognizing that glory for any of our accomplishments goes to God.

It is not rude, snapping at spouse or children when things don't go my way. It doesn't always want to have the house at my preferred temperature or eat at only my favorite restaurants. It is not easily angered at perceived or real injustices and keeps no record of all the times my husband sleeps while I get up with the baby or take the junior high student to early basketball practice.

Love doesn't rejoice over someone else's marital discord, but rejoices when truth and commitment win out. It always protects the smallest, sweetest confidences of its family members, always trusts, believing the best. It always hopes in the freshness of tomorrow, the great goodness of God, and the bright future of the family. It always perseveres in the face of hardship and doubt. It refuses to give up or surrender the commitment made in the company of God and friends.

Where there are sleepless, newborn nights, they shall end. Where there are diapers, mounting bills, too much month at the end of the money, soccer carpools, little league tournaments, and endless dioramas all built from shoeboxes, all due tomorrow, they will cease.

Where there are parent-teacher conferences, school programs, late night giggles, and slumberless sleepovers, they will be stilled. Where there is knowledge of buried trivia for school reports, Dr. Spock, Dr. Phil, Dr. Dobson, and Chapman's *Love Languages*, it will all pass away.

And now these three remain: **faith** to practice ourselves and instill in our children, and by doing so, in our grandchildren; **hope** that we survive child-rearing to celebrate a golden wedding anniversary and that our children will aspire to achieve great dreams; and **love** that illusive feeling, but concrete action, that covers a multitude of grouchy, less-than-perfect parenting and spousal moments. Love that makes memories, celebrates life, and remembers that people are more important than things. And the greatest of these is love.

It is what remains. Long after I am gone.

CHOCOLATE-COVERED QUESTIONS

1. What area of our married life do you think has changed the most in a negative way since the advent of our children?

2. What are the positive ways children have enhanced our marriage and brought us closer together?

3. Proverbs 17:6 says, "Children's children are a crown to the aged, and parents are the pride of their children." Are you looking forward to our days as grandparents? Why or why not?

4. Do you feel like I back you on discipline decisions? What do you think is a good plan for when we disagree?

5. How are being a father and a mother different (tasks, attitudes, characteristics)? The same?

6. Read Cindy's description of their anniversary cruise. What objections do you usually make to getting away alone together? Do both of you believe that such time is vital to the health of your marriage? For your part of your next date time, bring a notebook and camp out in front of the travel magazine section at your nearest bookstore. Dream about a getaway and then make concrete plans. Start building anticipation and excitement together.

SCRIPTURE

"Sons are a heritage from the LORD,
children a reward from him" (Psalm 127:3).

HOT CHOCOLATE TOPIC

Do you feel like our family is marriage-centered or child-centered? Why? What is one thing I could do to improve my focus on our relationship?

GOODNIGHT KISS

With God's help, I pledge to put our relationship as husband and wife before the children and other earthly priorities.

IS IT BETTER TO BE SINGLE OR MARRIED?

It's better for girls to be single, but not for boys. Boys need someone to clean up after them.

ANITA, AGE 9

Better Than Chocolate
Sexual Intimacy

*Seventy percent of women in a recent survey said they
would rather have chocolate than sex.*

REDBOOK, FEBRUARY 2007

I f you merely glanced at the above quote, read it again. As you
already know, I'm all for chocolate. Love it. Need it. Crave it. But
I want us to change this statistic, or at least not make it true for our
own marriages. Guess who invented sex? God. Okay, you knew that
one. But do you fully embrace that it is His holy, passionate, and really
fun idea? It's a hard concept for some of us to wrap our modest little
minds around, isn't it? First of all, we're not so comfortable with the
idea of God knowing that we do that (some of you are covering this
part of the page with your hand, aren't you?), and we tend to think God
is too serious for fun, for pleasure, and for delight. He created it!

When teaching the chapter on adolescence in my high school sociology classes, I told my students that on average boys think about sex
approximately once every eight seconds. Later, of course, we would
discuss the naturalness of this phenomenon and the absolute value
of waiting until marriage. They took it all in with an amazing amount
of respect, but as they exited to the halls, I could always hear my precious juniors and seniors counting 1-2-3-4-5-6-7-8 and collapsing in
peals of laughter.

It doesn't really change so much as boys mature into men. Christian humorist Dave Meurer puts it this way:

> Even as women are unfairly caricaturing us guys as having the sex drive of hyperactive weasels (At this point Meurer breaks for a funny footnote: "For the record, the *Journal of the American Medical Association* has documented that men have the sex drive of hyperactive ferrets, not weasels. So there."), we men are quietly going about the daily business of doing our jobs, taking care of the lawn, paying bills, getting the tires rotated, and engaging in a host of other productive activities, in many cases going an entire five minutes without thinking about sex, which proves we are not obsessed with this topic, but merely very, very interested in it. (That's "very" to the twenty-fourth power.)[1]

Dr. Kevin Leman phrases it this way, "If you want a normal husband, you're going to get one who thinks about sex a lot." Sex plays an enormously critical role in a healthy marriage. Research, practical experience, and anecdotal evidence (survey responses) all support the necessity of physical intimacy in marriage. Although sex sometimes fulfills different needs in a man than a woman, it's still crucial for the health of any marriage. No avoiding, no sidestepping. There's a reason for the timeworn cliché that a good wife needs to be an angel at home and a devil in bed.

I feel so blessed to have had an extraordinarily open relationship with my parents. So open in fact that when my mother was looking at the snapshots we had taken while on our honeymoon, she came to one of Greg in a hotel room in Dallas, leaning back in a leather recliner, arms behind his head and commented, "That looks like a *very* satisfied man!"

"Mother!" I scolded.

"If you're wise, you'll keep it that way."

I'd like to echo this challenge, "Let's not settle for enough sex so that our husbands stop bugging us. Let's get the whole works."[2] Ready? Let's get ready to study a really fun subject! Put on your cozy flannel jammies (perhaps for the last time!), grab a pencil, a highlighter, or a crayon and choose some things you know your husband would love. Sex isn't the only way we can bless our husbands, but we are the only ones who can bless them in this way.

Bedtime Bliss

Create your own cozy bedtime ritual. Tuck the kids in bed together. Then meet around the kitchen table, in front of the fireplace, or on the porch swing. Enjoy a cup of decaf coffee, tea, or a mug of hot cocoa together as you chat about your day. If your kids are older, take a walk around the neighborhood. Read a book together aloud. Pray. Take turns reading Scripture. Try a variety of things and find out what works best for you.

Remember, your husband is a visual creature.

I have addressed this critical point in a few of my other books, but it's worth repeating here. Men are turned on by sight, but some of us are dressing like we inherited amnesia around year three of marriage! I am reminded of a precious older lady in her 80s whom I met while speaking in Arizona. She waited to speak with me after the conference, her eyes gleaming mischievously.

"Sweetie, I just wanted to tell you another marriage story. My husband always said I had the best legs!" She paused to giggle girlishly. "The last year we were able to go away together, I was 78 years old and he was still going on about my legs. Isn't that something?" she marveled. Indeed.

Every night, much to my amazement after 12 years of marriage, my husband lies in wait after my shower. I go in our bedroom to put on lotion and jammies. He leers happily and calls it "The Show."

Instead of being aggravated, what about being grateful that your husband still wants you? There's a good reason that strip club revenues are generating enough income to fund third-world countries!

Since individual preferences vary greatly, ask your husband if he likes you to wear more makeup or less makeup. When you go on dates, would he like you best in blue jeans or in a feminine dress?

Body image seems to be a big hurdle for women when it comes to sex, especially after bearing children. According to a *Ladies' Home Journal* poll, even though 77 percent of women suspected that they worried about losing their looks more than their husbands did, they still worry. They think their thighs are too big. Their stretch marks are too, well, stretchy. Their breasts are too small. Too saggy.

Naked? They think, shrieking silently. *What's wrong with just hiking up the flannel nightgown a tad?*

Well, plenty. If you haven't caught on by now, guys are visual creatures. Just glimpsing a hint of skin, while we put on our pajamas before crawling into bed or a hint of cleavage as we fasten our bra in the morning, can be enough to initiate a personal fireworks show!

For those of you who refuse to contemplate anything other than the missionary position, feeling that your posterior gets buried in the mattress and sucking your stomach mattressward shows off your abs of styrofoam to better advantage, I have good news for you: Your husband is not thinking of all those things. Instead, he's celebrating the true meaning of the phrase "getting lucky." He's feeling genuinely lucky to be alone with a naked woman who is going to invite him to get as close and intimate to someone as you can possibly get.

On the surveys for this book, the most common response listed under what inhibits physical intimacy in your marriage (after stress and time) was the same for both sexes: appearance. The men said the frequency and quality of their sex lives were affected by the way their wives felt about their bodies. More than one man stated outright that their sex life was adversely affected by this simple statement, "She feels ugly, fat, or undesirable." The women would write (and it seemed as though you could almost see the downcast posture in their penmanship), "The way I look."

I have a friend whom I admire very much. Prior to knowing Jesus her husband worked as a videographer for *Playboy*. I think I'd be so intimidated it might border on neurotic! However, she is not in the least bit that way. She has the most wonderful smile and laid-back demeanor. She might not be the conventional definition of gorgeous, but she is because of *who* she is. Her husband is obviously in love with her. Most men confirm that confidence is sexy—complaining that you feel fat and gross, is not.

Remember, your husband is a sexual creature.

So are you. God made you that way. Don't sigh or roll your eyes when your husband approaches you for physical intimacy or make comments about how he just had some last night, for goodness sake, and doesn't he realize how very tired you are.

Of those men I surveyed who listed something they'd like to change about their sex lives, there were only two answers: frequency (one man followed that up by writing, "I bet that's an original response!") and the wish that their wives would *initiate* sex more often rather than making them feel like they were always having to beg permission.

Sex is as necessary as breathing for most men. They crave it and, because of the periodic buildup of seminal fluid, they actually *need* that release. In addition, for many men sex is the number one way of feeling close to you; that may be exactly their prescription for stress relief after a long hard day.

Remember the adage, "Women need a reason, men just need a place!" I've said it before and I'll repeat it here. Sex isn't close to even 20 percent of what makes a marriage successful; however, it does seem to be a fairly accurate barometer of the overall health of the relationship. Furthermore, research suggests that there is a direct correlation between the frequency of sex and the satisfaction with the quality of the relationship.

Be fully present for the act of love.

Men consider the sexual act as a gift of their love to you. They don't have one bit of a problem with the 1 Corinthians 7 admonition not to withhold your body from your spouse! One man put it like this:

I don't think men struggle with giving authority of their body to their wives. You want authority? Take it. It's yours. Do whatever you want, once, twice. Given the chance, we would gladly submit authority of our bodies to our wives in the morning, afternoon, evening, and middle of the night and twice on Sunday, Tuesday, and Thursday. I think this is one of the mysteries that men battle with. Why don't women have this same attitude?[3]

Consider this widely circulated letter from a husband's perspective.

To My Loving Wife:

During the past year I have tried to make love to you 365 times. I have succeeded only 36 times; an average of once every ten days. Following is a list of reasons why I did not succeed more often: it was too late, too early, too hot or too cold. It would awaken the children, the company in the next room or the neighbors whose windows were open. You were too full, had a headache, a backache, a toothache or the giggles. You pretended to be asleep or were not in the mood. You had on your mudpack. You watched the late TV show, or I did, or the baby was crying.

During the times I did succeed, the activity was not entirely satisfying for a variety of reasons. On six occasions you chewed gum the whole time; every so often you watched TV. Frequently you told me to hurry up and get it over with. A few times I tried to awaken you to tell you we were through, and once I was afraid I had hurt you for I hadn't felt you move.

We've had mercy sex, I want another child sex, I want a new sofa sex, guilt sex, and maintenance sex. Honey, it's no wonder I drink too much!

Your Loving Husband[4]

Educate yourself with Christian resources on sex.

On the bottom bookshelf in my dad's office, along with the rest of his marriage and counseling books, was a little paperback volume entitled *The Act of Marriage*, by Tim and Beverly LaHaye (yes, he's since added the Left Behind series to his repertoire). My mother jokingly referred to it as "Christian pornography" with simple pen-and-ink drawings. Nevertheless, I remember sneaking a look at this book one time when my parents were away.

Although most of us are acquainted with the basic mechanics of sex, there are many fabulous Christian resources available. Why Christian? It's not that there aren't good sex books out there on the secular market, but I much prefer to rely on those that are written from God's standpoint and view sex as right and pure only within the context of marriage.

We can become so caught up in our routines or our past beliefs about sex that we don't even notice how we relate to our partner sexually. The questionnaire I have created will help you explore what you like and what you don't like. Don't be embarrassed and don't let shame become part of the marriage bed. Give yourself time with these questions and be honest. God created the sexual union for this loving, committed relationship. Embrace it.

I recommend that you and your husband each complete the questionnaire individually. Then, discuss it *out* of the bedroom when you have plenty of time and are feeling close enough to be vulnerable and gently honest with each other. This is perfect to do on your annual getaway.

INTIMACY DISCUSSION TOOL

1. The material atmosphere and surroundings of our bedroom are important to me.
   Strongly Agree   Agree   No Opinion   Disagree   Strongly Disagree

2. I feel that our libido is compatibly matched.
   Strongly Agree   Agree   No Opinion   Disagree   Strongly Disagree

3. I feel comfortable talking about sexual issues with my spouse.
   Strongly Agree   Agree   No Opinion   Disagree   Strongly Disagree

4. I consider the physical attractiveness of my spouse to be of critical importance to our intimacy.

Strongly Agree   Agree   No Opinion   Disagree   Strongly Disagree

5. The husband should take the primary lead in sexual activities.

Strongly Agree   Agree   No Opinion   Disagree   Strongly Disagree

6. The wife has equal responsibility in initiating sexual encounters.

Strongly Agree   Agree   No Opinion   Disagree   Strongly Disagree

7. I would enjoy role play or appropriate fantasies in our lovemaking.

Strongly Agree   Agree   No Opinion   Disagree   Strongly Disagree

8. I would feel comfortable incorporating role play or appropriate fantasies in our lovemaking.

Strongly Agree   Agree   No Opinion   Disagree   Strongly Disagree

9. I am confident that I know how to satisfy my spouse sexually.

Strongly Agree   Agree   No Opinion   Disagree   Strongly Disagree

10. I feel that orgasm is the primary pleasure of lovemaking.

Strongly Agree   Agree   No Opinion   Disagree   Strongly Disagree

11. Feeling connected is the primary pleasure of lovemaking to me.

Strongly Agree   Agree   No Opinion   Disagree   Strongly Disagree

12. When our sex life is satisfying, I feel more satisfied with other areas in our marriage.

Strongly Agree   Agree   No Opinion   Disagree   Strongly Disagree

13. I am comfortable with my body image during lovemaking.

Strongly Agree   Agree   No Opinion   Disagree   Strongly Disagree

14. Procreation is the primary purpose of lovemaking.

Strongly Agree   Agree   No Opinion   Disagree   Strongly Disagree

15. After sex I like to have conversation.

Strongly Agree   Agree   No Opinion   Disagree   Strongly Disagree

16. After sex I like to cuddle.

    Strongly Agree   Agree   No Opinion   Disagree   Strongly Disagree

17. After sex I like to sleep.

    Strongly Agree   Agree   No Opinion   Disagree   Strongly Disagree

18. A healthy sex life is critical to a sense of play in marriage.

    Strongly Agree   Agree   No Opinion   Disagree   Strongly Disagree

19. I like to vary positions in lovemaking.

    Strongly Agree   Agree   No Opinion   Disagree   Strongly Disagree

20. I like to *initiate* new positions in lovemaking.

    Strongly Agree   Agree   No Opinion   Disagree   Strongly Disagree

21. My perspective on sex is healthy and mature.

    Strongly Agree   Agree   No Opinion   Disagree   Strongly Disagree

22. My perspective on sex is biblically based.

    Strongly Agree   Agree   No Opinion   Disagree   Strongly Disagree

23. I enjoy giving my spouse oral sex.

    Strongly Agree   Agree   No Opinion   Disagree   Strongly Disagree

24. I enjoy receiving oral sex as part of our lovemaking.

    Strongly Agree   Agree   No Opinion   Disagree   Strongly Disagree

25. These are the factors that most affect the quality or frequency of our lovemaking (circle all that apply).

    past experience   lack of experience   children   lack of time
    lack of sleep   lack of desire

26. I am satisfied with the number of times we make love each week.

    Strongly Agree   Agree   No Opinion   Disagree   Strongly Disagree

27. Visual stimulation is important to me.

    Strongly Agree   Agree   No Opinion   Disagree   Strongly Disagree

28. Romantic closeness is important to me.

    Strongly Agree   Agree   No Opinion   Disagree   Strongly Disagree

29. I would be willing to make love in a variety of locations pro-
    vided there was appropriate privacy.

    Strongly Agree   Agree   No Opinion   Disagree   Strongly Disagree

30. Pornography has no place in Christian lovemaking.

    Strongly Agree   Agree   No Opinion   Disagree   Strongly Disagree

31. Each of you note any of your unique differences that need to be
    discussed and negotiated.

    _____

    _____

    _____

    _____

If you set the mood and reserve the time to lovingly talk about
this, you may be happily surprised to embark on some of the best sex
you've had yet! The most wonderful thing about this tool, books like
this one, and devotionals like *Nightlight for Couples* (James and Shirley Dobson) is that they originate discussions you might otherwise
not have initiated and neither partner gets blamed for bringing up
touchy subjects because the authors have done it for you!

Never use sex as a bargaining tool.

Though the national average for the number of times married couples engage in sex is reportedly 2 to 2.3 times a week (I've had all kinds
of fun trying to figure out what that .3 includes), recent studies have
shown that couples who have sex 4 times a week look nearly a decade
younger! I promptly went upstairs and told my husband that for the
sake of doing accurate research, we probably better try it out.

Nevertheless, I am consistently shocked by the number of women
who report withholding sex as punishment or as a means of getting
something they want. One woman actually shared with me that she
told her husband she'd never sleep with him again unless he let her
have another baby! I was appalled. I can't imagine how he felt.

Walking through the halls at one conference, I heard a group of women giggling about it. I guess they got what they wanted—the new couch, the nice vacation. But I wonder what it cost in terms of intimacy. You see, most men feel close to you emotionally when they're close to you physically. It is a comfortable way for them to express the depth of their feelings for you. On the surveys, many men responded that the lack of sex inhibited emotional intimacy in their marriage, while the presence of sex increased emotional intimacy. One man wrote a single word for what increased physical intimacy in his marriage—weekends!

On the other hand, using sex as a reward for something (when it's all in fun and both parties know it) can be fun. Kevin Leman tells a story about a woman whose husband hated shopping. (Wait a minute—isn't that *all* of us?) He had tagged along with her to many stores and when she pleaded to make one last stop at Target, he nearly hit the roof. She promised him it would be the last place he had to go in and then leaned over and whispered in his ear what his reward would be when they got home. He cheerfully went into the store with her and now they refer to whatever it was she promised him as the "Target Special"! Perhaps we need to invent a Target Special of our own.

Let's be clear about something though. Sex should never, *never* be something your husband feels he has to earn. It should always be graciously and warmly given. It is a precious gift to be mutually shared and enjoyed.

> "*True love requires some consistently hard decisions.*"
> M. Scott Peck

Adjust your expectations.

In my studies of writing, I find many category romances to be, well...lame, but there is a market for them because we crave romance. I see women snatching them up every week like health food at my local grocery store. But I want to caution against thinking that every lovemaking session can be like those in books, even the catastrophically silly ones.

> *Gradually they drew together, their bodies complementing each other.*
>
> *She felt like someone who had been stranded in the desert too long without water.*
>
> *Her thirst for him increased with each wild kiss, and she inched herself ever closer to him, straining toward the river of fulfillment she sensed in the distance.*[5]

If that were the best example of writing in the world, it would still prompt an outbreak of guffaws. It just doesn't seem to match real life. At least *my* life. If I were to write such a paragraph, it might read like this:

> *Wearily, she suppresses a sigh as she slips out of her baby food stained overalls. He hears her come into the room and instantly clicks off the nightly news. She knows that once they get started, it will be fine. Her husband is a tender and considerate lover. She returns his ardent and passionate kisses with tentatively increasing passion as she listens to the baby monitor and wonders if she remembered to lock the door. Afterward, she lies in his arms, desperately thirsty, too tired to go downstairs and get a drink. Besides, that reminds her, did she remember to pick up more milk at the store? Sigh. Dry cereal tomorrow.*

That said, there are times that soulful, satisfying sex with your husband is the private equivalent of what would be a best-seller!

Husband Helper

> *Did you know that while sex nearly always results in orgasm for the male, it isn't always necessary for your wife in order for her to feel sexually fulfilled? This is not to say she doesn't enjoy them, but the cuddling and attention from you are often just as big a draw.*

Chocolate-Covered Questions

1. Which answer best describes how often you'd like to have sex every week?

    1-2 times   3-4 times   5-6 times   7 or more

2. If our answers differ, how could we compromise to be more in sync, but still make sure our needs are met?

3. Obtain a copy of Joseph Dillow's *Solomon on Sex* and take the Lover's Quotient test.

4. Choose one of the Christian books on sex and study it together as a couple. Re-rank your love life at the end of the study!

Scripture

"The husband should fulfill his marital duty to his wife, and likewise the wife to her husband. The wife's body does not belong to her alone but also to her husband. In the same way, the husband's body does not belong to him alone but also to his wife. Do not deprive each other except by mutual consent and for a time, so that you may devote yourselves to prayer. Then come together again so that Satan will not tempt you because of your lack of self-control" (1 Corinthians 7:3-5).

Hot Chocolate Topic

Dr. Dobson has said that if a man wants an exciting sexual relationship with his wife, he should be paying lots of attention to the other 23½ hours in the day.

Goodnight Kiss

Honey, tonight my body is all yours. What would you like to do?

HOW WOULD THE WORLD BE DIFFERENT
IF PEOPLE DIDN'T GET MARRIED?

There sure would be a lot of kids to explain, wouldn't there?

KELVIN, AGE 8

Unwrapping Love's Delights
Setting the Mood

*Girls ought to be more modest, and wives ought to
be less so—around their husbands. Instead, single women
show thighs and breasts, and wives dress like Eskimos.*

<small>BOB, FROM DR. LAURA'S BOOK</small>
THE PROPER CARE AND FEEDING OF HUSBANDS

In the last chapter I was pretty specific. Maybe you're still blushing. Believe me, as you explore the wonder of a healthy sex life, it becomes a great gift for you and your husband. If you feel life is too crazy to add more things to your plate, start simply.

Remember that while we long for our husbands to be more open and sensitive spirited with us, they're "only sensitive when (they) feel safe and when (their) sexual needs are met."[1]

Let's explore ways to increase the intimacy in your marriage by setting the mood and creating a place of sanctuary in your life, your home, and your bedroom. Unwrap the delicious gift of intimacy, freedom, vulnerability, honesty, and connection with the love of your life.

Bedroom Blues

Your bedroom can often end up becoming a catchall room—a laundry repository, a makeshift office, baby nursery (they really do need their own room after three months; go ahead and buy the ultra cool monitor instead), junk room, scrapbook central station. Sound familiar? It might take some major cleaning efforts to turn your bedroom back into a place for soul-sharing sex, heartfelt conversation, and energy-renewing sleep, but it will be worth it.

Begin with your closet. Try on everything you have and make three piles: keep, give away or garage sale, and throw away. Next, tackle the stacks. Throw away dusty pieces of mail, old magazines, and unmatched socks from that growing colony underneath your bed. View your bedroom with a critical eye and remove five items that are making it appear cluttered or dated.

> *"Couples who have a television in the bedroom have sex only half as often as those who don't, finds a new study."*
> LADIES' HOME JOURNAL, APRIL 2006

Revamp the atmosphere of your love nest. Solicit your husband's help in choosing colors and patterns that include him, making a cozy respite for the two of you without making it look too girly. Your bedroom is not the place to display cute pictures of the kids or to tack up the sweet drawings they've made in school. Paint is the cheapest makeover. Consider adding a border, stencils, a well-chosen picture, or a chair rail. Reserve some space for him to display treasures that are uniquely his. Above Greg's chest of drawers is a shelf with the pewter Star Trek Enterprise replica that I gave him at our rehearsal dinner, a fun picture of the two of us, and a hand-framed copy of our wedding invitation. It manages to be manly and sentimental at the same time.

Concentrate on your bed. Is it time for a new one? Invest in a really great mattress. Include a fluffy comforter or duvet cover for the colder months, a quilt for the warmer months, and a down mattress cover for extra cushion and coziness. Have on hand at least one set of beautiful matched sheets. Lightly scent them with a lavender or vanilla linen spray.

Consider piles of pillows for reading and lounging. Most decorating experts recommend at least two pillows per person. Shams and throw pillows add to the look. Make sure you have reading lamps, candles, fresh flowers, and a light throw for nap times. A colored bulb or dimmer switch lights will add to the ambience.

Bedroom Themes

Here are some ideas to get you started. Choose a theme that suits you both...or that you think will inspire you both.

Arabian Nights

- ♥ Four-poster bed
- ♥ Drape canopy with sheer fabric in coordinating colors
- ♥ Tack clear lights around the ceiling
- ♥ Choose silky bedding coordinates in rich jewel tones
- ♥ Place glow-in-the-dark stars in patterns on a ceiling that's painted blue

Cottage Garden

- ♥ Canopy bed in whitewash finish (or nail a piece of picket fencing to the wall behind a bed frame to make your own garden look)
- ♥ Draw tab panel curtains around the canopy rail; make coordinating tie-backs for daytime
- ♥ Place an assortment of real and silk plants and trees in room corners
- ♥ Paint window trim and molding in fresh white to contrast with whatever paint color you choose for the walls
- ♥ Use that quilt you received as a wedding present with a simple white or eyelet bed skirt
- ♥ Choose one striking Amish or uncluttered outdoor scene to frame and hang

Log Cabin

- ♥ Any rustic bed will do: antique, pine, deep oak
- ♥ Consider wallpapering some of your walls with a realistic looking brick, wood, or log paper
- ♥ Choose quilted bedding in classic country colors (navy, red, white, hunter green) and add accessories with gingham or stripes
- ♥ Choose primitive lodge look or cowboy themed accessories (be careful not to make it look like a children's room with that last one)
- ♥ Hanging lanterns or old pitchers converted into lamps are an especially nice touch
- ♥ Use a soft braided rug to anchor the room
- ♥ Complete the look by installing swinging café doors to separate the toilet section of the bathroom from the rest of the room

Seaside Escape

- ♥ Use blended paint ranging in hues from turquoise to misty blue and sponge paint clouds on walls near ceilings
- ♥ Choose crisp white or soft pastels in buttery yellows, sky blues, and ocean greens for bedding
- ♥ Attach a length of rope netting to the wall and affix some of the seashells you collected on your honeymoon for a 3-D touch
- ♥ Fill small jars with sand to use as votive holders
- ♥ Consider using a screen door to replace the door to the adjoining master bath
- ♥ Check out the tromp l'oeil wallpaper scenes and see if any would fit your rooms dimensions
- ♥ Place soft throw rugs at the sides of the bed

"Sex is not an event—it's an environment."
LINDA DILLOW AND LORRAINE PINTUS IN *INTIMATE ISSUES*

I have seen a beautifully decorated train-themed room saved from being overly masculine by feminine touches of a church pew bench, wild flowers in mason jars, and baskets for storage.

My neighbor has done a fantastic job of making their bedroom into a jungle retreat by blending various animal skin patterns, African artifacts, statues, pottery, animal prints, and even a mirror with a simple African art border. They got the idea from a beautiful silhouette made entirely of butterfly wings that was sent to them by a friend who was in Africa for the Peace Corps. The piece was so well-loved it became the basis for an entire room.

Browse through decorating magazines for other good ideas that reflect your tastes. Watch for sales, such as $29.99 for any size quilt or the bed-in-a-bag sets. Italian fashion designer Luisa Beccaria says, "If your bed looks beautiful, the whole room will look beautiful." Karen Scalf Linamen states it in terms that are a bit more down to earth, "Aim for *Southern Living* in your private quarters even if the rest of your house looks like *Mechanics Weekly*."[2] Isn't that just the perfect mental picture?

Bedroom Checklist

- ♥ Comfortable mattress
- ♥ Décor is uncluttered and aesthetically pleasing to both of us
- ♥ Lovely, but not overly frilly comforter or quilt
- ♥ Many decorating experts recommend at least two pillows per person
- ♥ Pillow shams, bolsters, decorative pillows
- ♥ Cozy throws for naps
- ♥ Candles
- ♥ Small CD player or iPod dock to set the mood and mask sounds from little (or not so little) ears
- ♥ Small table and chairs for late night romantic meal, popcorn snacks, or games of strip checkers

- ♥ Throw rugs for warming feet at the side of the bed

- ♥ Soft lighting or adjustable lights (try a colored bulb, a dimmer switch, or individual reading lamps)

- ♥ Ceiling fan to regulate room temperature

- ♥ Mattress topper—quilted, down, or down-substitute for hotel quality comfort

- ♥ Twinkling glow-in-the-dark stars for the ceiling

- ♥ Try sheets in a variety of textures: flannel, cotton, satin (One caution there—always pair either the fitted sheet or the top sheet with one from a non-satin set. Using the whole satin sheet set, pillows and all, is an invitation for one of you to go flying off the bed at very inopportune times!)

- ♥ Lock on the bedroom door

- ♥ No unnecessary household clutter, juvenile items, and other unrestful stuff

- ♥ Inviting baskets of reading material

- ♥ A small bench or oversized wing chair for reading, relaxing, putting on your shoes, or just sitting and daydreaming

What Is Okay in the Marriage Bed?

If it were possible to bottle and market my parents' formula, I would do it. Somehow they managed to convince my sister and me that sexual activity outside of marriage was not only very wrong, it would harm our relationships with our future someday husbands. Yet after the wedding, neither of us had any hang-ups nor felt that marital intimacy was in any way dirty. We entered into marriage with a wonderful innocence, a healthy curiosity, and a biblical perspective on sex.

I know from talking to hundreds of women, however, that all

of us weren't blessed with such an experience. Some of us grew up being taught that sex was a chore, a duty expected of us in marriage. Others experienced this act that was meant to be enjoyed within the boundaries of marriage under less than ideal circumstances.

Carley was raised on a farm and knew all about the mechanics of sex, but her mother explained it to her as a painful, humiliating task to be endured. Consequently, her wedding night did not result in the act of love, and it was years before she gave herself to her husband without inhibition.

Helen was sexually abused by several trusted friends and family members as a child. As a result, she dreaded sex, could not relax enough to reach orgasm, and secretly thought of lovemaking as "dirty."

RaeAnn was also sexually abused as a child. She responded by dressing provocatively and behaving promiscuously during high school and college. She brought tremendous guilt with her into the bedroom.

Johnna is a beautiful, young woman, but she can't get past the fact that she was a virgin on her wedding night, but her husband, Jake, was not. Sex has become miserable for her because she constantly wonders if she's being compared to Jake's other lovers.

Clearly, our vastly different backgrounds and experiences shape a broad continuum of attitudes toward sex. Obviously, there is no single book that can magically erase years of abuse or a painful, traumatic experience. I urge you to seek help from a trusted Christian counselor if you have any marital issue that does not seem to improve.

~

There are certain guidelines that God has set forth in His Word that can help all of us, regardless of our current attitudes toward marital intimacy.

Taking Every Thought Captive

Second Corinthians 10:5 exhorts us, "Take captive every thought to make it obedient to Christ." Beth Moore calls this "re-wallpapering." In Christ we are all new creatures. Whatever the sin or hurt in our past has been forgiven. Ask for God's help to transform your mind (Romans 12:2) and bring it into line with His original design.

Pray about sex. Be honest with God about your misgivings. Thank Him for inventing this marvelous gift. Ask Him to remind you that within marriage, sex is not only permissible, but blessed and fun! Beseech Him to fill you with desire for your husband and to give you a spirit of bedroom adventure while you're at it!

Pray during sex. If your mind fills up with old fantasies or pictures during lovemaking with your husband, ask God to transfer your thoughts elsewhere. Ask Him to keep your mind in the moment.

Prepare for sex. It's quite the transition to make from mommy to sex goddess after reading about Olivia the pig to the toddler, rocking the baby, throwing in one more load of laundry, putting the dishwasher on delay, and making a final sweep through the house. Take a few moments to breathe deeply, shower or bathe, perhaps add lipstick, and choose to wear something you know your husband will admire.

Throughout the day, fantasize about your husband in a sexual way. Think about the things you admire about him. Call him at work to let him know what you're thinking.

Carefully and prayerfully examine your attitudes about sex. My friend Kate once asked me, "If it's something I know I won't like, do I have to try it anyway?" While neither partner should pressure the other into doing something they don't feel comfortable with, my answer is that if it doesn't violate any of the guidelines (we'll discuss these a bit later in the chapter), then yes, try it one or two times to give it an honest chance. You may find out it's more fun than you thought!

If not, don't dismiss your husband's desires. Just respectfully say, "Honey, I didn't really enjoy doing that, but I really do want to please you. What about this?" Fill in the blank with a compromise or an idea of your own.

Other than requesting an increase in frequency, the second most common request that I saw on surveys (and that I hear when I'm speaking) is for the wife to be more aggressive in sex; to initiate the encounter sometimes. Variety isn't just a necessity in the kitchen, it's critical in the bedroom too.

Linda Dillow has said that while we would never consider serving the same, ordinary, microwaved meal night after night, many women serve the same, lukewarm, ordinary sex night after night in the bedroom.

Each of us is different in our level of confidence, our backgrounds, and our styles. I wouldn't presume to tell you that you should definitely incorporate a certain act or outfit or anything else in the bedroom, but perhaps you could adapt a few ideas from this chapter to suit your style and wow your husband!

Inhibition Inhibitors

- ♥ Search out and purchase some lingerie in which you feel comfortable.

- ♥ Bathe together in bubbles by candlelight together as a prelude to lovemaking.

- ♥ Exercise your PC muscles (the vaginal muscles that you contract to stop the flow of urine). Exercise. If you feel overweight, it will show in your bedroom confidence level. And if you truly are, a loss of as little as five pounds promotes better sleep, takes stress off your joints, and revs up your energy.

- ♥ Remember that it is truly a compliment that your husband desires you and wants to see you naked!

"Taking joy in living is a woman's best cosmetic."
ROSALIND RUSSELL

Beauty Boosters

- ♥ Contract your abdominal muscles tightly to the count of 25 every hour.

- ♥ Rinse your hair with vinegar and cool water occasionally for a shine boost.

- ♥ Use an exfoliator in the shower at least twice a week.

- ♥ For really dry skin, smooth a light film of baby oil on slightly damp skin and then follow with your favorite lotion.

- ♥ For maximum impact, layer fragrances: body wash, lotion, powder, perfume.

- ♥ Drink water. We often mistake thirst for hunger signals. Slip eight rubber bands on your wrist in the morning and remove one for each glass of water you consume.

- ♥ Even if you're not a big makeup person, at least wear tinted moisturizer with SPF 15 to even out and protect your skin and a softly tinted lip gloss for moisture, protection, and color.

- ♥ A satin pillowcase is easier on your hair and skin; less muss and fewer wrinkles.

The Idea Cache for Hot Chocolate Fun

- ♥ Instead of an 18-hour bra, try 18-hour foreplay. Begin the day with a warm cuddle and a few well-placed kisses. Put on a show for him while you're getting into your bra and underwear set that morning. Buy some glass chalk or window markers and leave him a coded message about what you'll be planning for later that night. Follow up with a playful email. Fantasize about him throughout the day so that you will be mentally prepared for your lovemaking session.

- ♥ If your husband travels a lot, consider instituting a miniature phone sex session right before he comes home. There must be a reason that 1-900 numbers are such a booming business, and lucky for your husband, his sex life is your very fun business!

♥ If your husband works an opposite shift or an extra long shift, don't let him leave without "servicing" him. Make sure that he leaves home feeling that he'd like to return as soon as possible for more loving.

♥ Anytime you need to borrow his car keys or some change, reach in his pocket and spend some time there.

♥ Place your hand high up on his thigh when you're snuggling together.

♥ Brush your breasts against his arm when you're pressed for space. Smile at him and say, "Excuse me!"

♥ Purchase a great Christian resource for study together. Note the pages you'd like to try and leave the book on his pillow.

♥ Wake him up in the middle of the night for sex. Set the alarm if you have to.

♥ Turn down your bed hotel style and set chocolate mints on the pillows.

♥ Put in a CD of upbeat music and model everything from swimsuits and lingerie to shirts and sexy underwear (go braless) on your own private bedroom "catwalk." Don't worry, the show won't last long.

♥ As a variation, let your husband choose your outfit and "pose" you, allowing him to be the pretend photographer.

♥ When you know you're meeting for a slow session of lovemaking, bring a cup of hot chocolate or a cup of crushed ice to bed (depending on the weather) and have fun using your imagination.

♥ Imitate the Shulamite maiden from Song of Solomon and do a special dance just for him. If you're very self-conscious, keep a length of sheer, gauzy fabric with you.

♥ A lap dance perhaps? If you're like me and you've never seen one either, I bet we could figure it out pretty quickly.

♥ The nooner! (My husband called me from an out of town instructional school he was attending. They drew words which could be taken a variety of ways from a hat and were required to do an extemporaneous speech. His word? Nooner. Reportedly, he used up his two minutes debating the pros and cons.)

♥ At the end of a hard day, ask him to unzip your dress. When it falls to the ground, turn around and press against him. Make sure you're wearing your most beautiful bra and underwear set.

♥ If he sits on the edge of the bed to get dressed, straddle him.

♥ While he's in the shower put a towel in the dryer. Greet him with it and offer a post-shower rub down.

♥ Go to Sam's Club or somewhere you can purchase fragrant roses at a less than astronomical price; sprinkle the rose petals all over your bed just before you make love. The texture and fragrance will make your evening extra special.

♥ Sometimes wear your high heels with your fancy nighties.

♥ Play "hypothermia" and sleep naked; just keep your bathrobes handy for any small late-night visitors.

♥ I had the privilege of speaking at the same Hearts at Home conference as Pam Farrell. She is hilarious and is extremely committed to spicing up marriages by making intimacy fun. Together with her husband, she wrote a book entitled *Red-Hot Monogamy*. I'll give her credit for this idea for hands-on homework: Spread oil or lotion on a brand-new shower curtain for a grown-up version of Slip-n-Slide!

♥ Next time your bedroom needs painting, paint it together without your clothes on (after the kids are down for the count). You'll save on laundry time later!

♥ Give yourself permission to think sexual thoughts about your husband. Do more than think about what a nice guy he is (although there is a place for that too). Actively fantasize about being intimate with him and let him know what you're thinking!

♥ Most men will find it a turn on for you to verbalize what you'd like him to do to you and what you're planning to do to him. This will take lots of practice for some of us; start slowly. A darkened room might be more comfortable as you first get used to the idea. Remember, he *is* your husband so what you do together is blessed.

♥ Consider an on-the-road adventure. Drive somewhere new. Find a secluded area and take a break in the back of the truck or spread a blanket on the grass.

♥ If it's just the two of you around the house, wear a thin T-shirt and go braless.

♥ Try candlelight. Its romantic shimmer is flattering to every body.

♥ Bring fruit, pretzels, and French bread into your bedroom, along with a fondue pot or one of those small chocolate fountains. Take turns feeding each other.

♥ How about adding a spray can of whipped cream to your grocery list? The possibilities are up to you!

♥ Try a new position, and you be the one to initiate it.

♥ Read the Song of Solomon aloud to each other.

♥ Buy something to wear in the bedroom besides that holey gray T-shirt you usually wear.

♥ If he has a private office at work, pop in for a surprise visit. Wear a business suit with nothing underneath. If your husband works construction, see if there's a private, deserted section of scaffolding you can utilize. Get creative!

♥ While you're out to dinner, inform him that you've "forgotten" to wear your underwear and then time how long it takes for him to signal for the check! (Check the wind factor forecast before attempting this one!)

♥ Play romantic music in your bedroom.

♥ Play strip poker. Strip checkers. Naked Twister.

♥ Be more aggressive.

♥ Make him a coupon booklet of fun favors he can use whenever he desires.

♥ Become acquainted with his perineum, that ultrasensitive spot behind the scrotum. Caress it gently with your fingertips.

♥ No matter how tired you feel, have sex every night for an entire week. You'll find that having sex begets the desire for more sex.

♥ I once read an ad that said, "Every woman should own one pair of jeans that can make a grown man cry." Go shopping, girlfriends!

♥ Make it your goal to "christen" every room of the house. My neighbor and friend Cheryl got a kick out of that suggestion. Last summer she and her husband built a beautiful brick patio off their backyard deck. The landscaping is private and inviting and the small lamps give off a welcoming glow. After a tour I brought her over a bottle of sparkling soda and a candle with instructions to make sure they christened that patio one night after the kids were all in bed. A few weeks later she reported, "My husband says to thank you for chapters like these!"

♥ Try a temporary tattoo. On a girlfriends' outing to the mall, I bought all four of us, in our late thirties and one forty-year-old, wives a rhinestone stick-on tattoo. We all pledged to use it within the week. Surrounding yourself with friends who will encourage you to fan the sparks in your marriage is essential. Invite your husband to play a different version of hide and seek. Tell him he needs to find the new item on your body.

♥ Neatly trim your bikini area. For the very brave, go for a wax. Your husband is guaranteed to notice and enjoy your new hair-cut.

♥ Get to know your husband and his preferences intimately. Make pleasing him sexually one of your greatest marital ambitions. As you talk, experiment, and study, make other additions to this list until you have a surefire repertoire of your own, complete with some fireworks surprises!

I wouldn't call her anyone's moral model, but Zsa Zsa Gabor was right on in her observation, "Husbands are like fires, they go out if unattended." I once heard a speaker say, "If you don't have an affair with your spouse, someone else will."

Kay Cole James, a wonderful Christian speaker and secretary of health under the Reagan/Bush administration, puts it this way, "Sister-girlfriends, the sad sorry truth of it is, if you're not giving your husband what he needs (sexually) there are women out there who will!" She adds with much love and laughter, "We need to *bless* the brothers!" It's true, you know. You are the only woman in the world with the right and privilege of blessing your husband in this delightful way!

～

I love the way my parents explained it to my sister and me before our weddings: Anything that is pleasurable to you both and harmful to neither is fair game! There are some things which obviously do not meet those criteria. In their excellent book *Intimate Issues,* Linda Dillow and Lorraine Pintus provide three questions to ask about any sexual practice you are considering:

Is it prohibited in Scripture?

If Scripture forbids it, then it's out. Period. "Everything is permissible for me" (1 Corinthians 6:12).

Is it beneficial?

Does the practice harm either of you (see the above general guidelines)? Does it hinder the sexual relationship between you? If the answer to either is yes, it should be rejected. "Everything is permissible for me—but not everything is beneficial" (1 Corinthians 6:12).

Does it involve anyone else?

Your sex life is a blessed and sacred activity between you and your spouse alone. If it involves another person or is seen by others, it is wrong. As Dillow and Pintus point out, based on these three sound questions, X-rated videos are out. Pornography is insidious in its addictive nature. In addition to being immoral and against God's law, "According to psychologist Douglas Kendrick's research, men shown pictures of Playboy models do later describe themselves as less in love with their wives than do men shown other images."[3] Besides all that, who needs false and unattainable standards held up as the "norm"? I would suggest that you and your husband pray over and carefully study any gray area that you are considering in the privacy of your lovemaking.

Ten Things God Forbids

1. *Fornication*—immoral sex; it stems from a Greek word *porneia,* which means unclean. We usually use it to mean sex outside of marriage (1 Corinthians 7:2).

2. *Adultery*—sex with someone other than your spouse; Jesus included emotional affairs in Matthew 5:28.

3. *Homosexuality*—God speaks strongly against this, calling it "detestable" to Him (Leviticus 18:22, 1 Corinthians 6:9, and others).

4. *Impurity*—broad term usually referring to general moral uncleanness (2 Corinthians 7:1).

5. *Orgies*—sex with multiple partners, which Scripture clearly condemns.

6. *Prostitution*—paying for sex; Leviticus 19:29 and the book of Proverbs are full of warnings against this and adultery.

7. *Lustful passions*—this does *not* refer to passion for your spouse (Ephesians 4:19).

8. *Sodomy*—an Old Testament word that refers to men lying with men. The English word incorporates that definition and adds to it, unnatural sexual intercourse and sex with an animal (bestiality). A colloquial use has sodomy referring to anal intercourse.

   (Note, although some Christian teachers place oral sex under this umbrella, they are in error. In fact, many

Christian scholars believe that the Song of Solomon refers to this act between husband and wife.)

9. *Obscenity and coarse jokes*—the Greek word for "unwholesome" means "rotten" or "decaying." Linda Dillow and Lorraine Pintus take care to note that this does not rule out appropriate sexual humor in the privacy of marriage (Ephesians 4:29).

10. *Incest*—sexual intercourse with family members or relatives (Leviticus 18:7-18; 20:11-21).[4]

If your husband wants to try something that doesn't violate any of those principles, then yes, I'd give it a *genuine* try. However, if you find that the request makes you feel incredibly uncomfortable, assure him of your love and your desire to spice things up and offer a compromise idea of your own.

If you've never before given it much thought, I'm sure by now you realize how important the sexual relationship is to your husband. However, "great sex, over the long term, doesn't mean much if the rest of the relationship is mediocre."[5] Respect, appreciation, fair fighting, and good communication are also necessary ingredients in the recipe for a great marriage. You don't have to be able to do back flips or even be able to spell Kama Sutra. What men are looking for in the bedroom is a confident, willing wife who welcomes her husband with her smile, her arms, her heart, and her body. And that, precious girlfriends, is who you are.

Husband Helper

Chances are your wife's senses are more heightened than your own. That means that foreplay has got to be more than brushing your teeth and dropping your jeans on the floor by the bed. Take another shower. Know that ragged, overgrown toenails aren't a turn on. If her delicate skin is sensitive, shave just for her.

CHOCOLATE-COVERED QUESTIONS

1. What could you change about the physical atmosphere of your bedroom and your bedtime habits that could increase your sexual intimacy and the feeling that your room is a refuge?

2. Does your husband feel you dress sexily enough to please him during private times together? If not, what could you do to improve?

3. According to the surveys, many husbands list their wife's perception of her body as a stumbling block to both the intensity and frequency of sexual intimacy. Is this a problem in your marriage? What could you do to be more accepting of your husband's desire for you? What could you do to improve your body image and your perception of it?

4. Together look over the list of what God prohibits in the sexual relationship. Are you in danger of violating any of those principles?

SCRIPTURE

"Unless the LORD builds the house,
its builders labor in vain" (Psalm 127:1).

HOT CHOCOLATE TOPIC

How can we make our bedroom more of a refuge? What is something you want us to try sometime? Tonight?

GOODNIGHT KISS

I want my heart, body, home, and life to be open to you.

The rule goes like this: If you kiss someone, then you should marry them and have kids with them. It's the right thing to do.

HOWARD, AGE 8

9

Protecting Your Chocolate
Boundaries for a Healthy Marriage

The way to get rid of ice is not to use a hammer, but to melt it.

<small>Eugenia Price in *The Waiting Time*</small>

When I present my marriage seminar, there are usually some where between 21 and 1500 women in an auditorium with their pencils poised over notebooks ready to get the most out of the conference experience. This section is the only one that attendees give as much attention to as the section with information on sex. What topic could possibly give sex a run for the money? Affair-proofing our marriages. Oh, that one!

I begin with the same statement every time. The best defense against an affair is to realize that no one's marriage is immune. *No one's.* We're tempted to blame temptation on all the stuff around us, but actually the seeds are right there within us. Under the right circumstances, given the right trigger, *anyone* is susceptible to cheating. Think about what kind of person, what kind of circumstances, what kind of vulnerabilities might make you act faithlessly. Then avoid even the appearance of such a scenario like the plague.

Why is the admission that this could happen to us so important? Because it takes the wind right out of the sails of those who might be complacent or would gloat, at least secretly, that such a thing would "never, ever happen" to them.

Remember our earlier discussion about the heart? Don't trust yourself. "Sexual feelings are, in great part, biological, and at times sexual desire can rush in when we aren't prepared for it. Never assume you (or any of your friends) are in complete control of these feelings—especially if you and your husband are not getting along well."[1]

How do you know when a relationship is crossing the line? "An extramarital tie of any kind has lost its 'cleanness' and 'neatness' the moment *any level of sexuality enters into it.*"[2]

Still think I might be overstating the case? Dr. Kevin Leman posed this exercise so that women might better understand the sexually oriented, visually impacted world of men. Think of a man that you trust and admire. He must be a nonrelative. "(I guarantee you don't want to hear this, but I [Leman] will tell it to you anyway.) You got this guy in your mind? Good. Now put yourself in a position where you're meeting this man in a social situation. In less than one-fifth of a second, this man has checked you out from your toes to your head and *all* major spots in between."[3] If you don't believe it, Leman suggests asking your husband. I did that one night and literally shivered. I tried to argue.

"You're kidding me!" I scolded my husband.

"Serious," he said in his verbose way. And my eyes were opened, perhaps for the first time ever, to exactly how sexual all men are.

One of my precious friends from college, a minister, has decided to reinvent himself. He lost weight, purchased an array of youthful-looking clothing, and left his family behind in pursuit of a thrilling new relationship with another woman. His children are resentful; his wife heartbroken.

This all seemed sudden, but in reality, it was not. It was months in the making. A gradual fogging of the transparent windows of his life. A decision to avoid tackling the hard issues with his wife. A deliberate distancing from friendships and time with God, both of which would have convicted him of wrong doing. The netherworld of his own creation is protecting him from feeling condemnation. If you were to ask him, he'll tell you he did the right thing.

Think this is unique? It's not. I have had countless Christian people tell me with straight faces that they believe God does not want them unhappy. They even credit God with having brought this new love into their lives! We can be involved in a Bible study, spouting off all the correct answers, and fall down hard. We think with certainty that the one area in which temptation would never touch us is our marriages, and we could be devastatingly wrong. Look around you. Such misconceptions are leaving behind wrecked relationships and broken promises every day.

Warning Signs

Before we start thinking men are the only ones running the risk of infidelity, remember that no relationship is immune, and no one person—of either gender—is immune. Consider some of these red-flag signals that might be flying in the innocent winds of preaffair conditions. You might be surprised to realize that you've seen a few of these flags flying over your own activities.

- ♥ I sometimes dress up or pay more attention to my appearance in the presence of this person.
- ♥ I enjoy trading sexual innuendos with this person.
- ♥ Sometimes I don't tell my spouse about conversations, emails, or meetings with this person.
- ♥ I spend longer than necessary finishing a conversation or relaying information to this person. Remember, the number one affair partner is someone you work with.
- ♥ I have discussed private marital struggles or personal issues with this person.
- ♥ Other activities are replacing my times with my husband.
- ♥ Images of this person sometimes creep into times of intimacy with my spouse.
- ♥ I am distancing myself from friends close enough to call me on my flirtatious behavior with this person.

♥ I sense a physical spark or intense connection whenever this person is close.

♥ I have a kind of radar and am able to locate this person quickly in a room.

♥ I've altered my routine so that I "accidentally" run into this person more often.

♥ I have hidden other things from my spouse—for example, the price of an item or the purchase of certain new things.

♥ I am allowing my friendship with this person to meet needs in me that should be met by my own husband.

♥ I find myself deliberately creating emotional distance from my spouse while being overly solicitous in other ways.

♥ I feel the need to justify my association with this person anytime I run into someone else or have a conversation about it.

It is vital to know these signs and check your heart against them periodically. Fudging in seemingly small areas of our marriage loosens our grip on the truth. The lure of an affair can be great, especially when we are in a period of disenchantment or disappointment in our marriages. "Any affair is an attempt to escape reality by pursuing a fantasy of some kind."[4] Thus, an affair is always an illusion. I can remember my daddy telling the couples he counseled, "The grass might be greener, but it still has to be mowed!" In fact, 75 percent of affair partners who marry end up divorced again.

We can face the truth that there is no readily available inoculation against divorce. So what *can* we do? We fall on our knees before the creator of marriage, acknowledge our weakness, affirm our desire to do right, and pray. We can also keep TABS on our marriage: transparency, accountability, boundaries.

Transparency

It is essential that we make sure that our lives and our beliefs match. Obviously we can't be perfect, but the minute we begin to hide information, fudge on facts, or tolerate tiny untruths, we're in big trouble. Once we lie, we are slaves to that lie, at least for a season.

This means taking the level of transparency in your life or marriage to a depth with which you're uncomfortable at first. Start with the basics. Simple honesty about everyday things. Keep your computer in an open area, easily accessible to the rest of the family. It's difficult to hide things in the open.

Prayerfully seek another couple with whom you can be transparent about your marriage. In her book *The Power of a Praying Wife*, Stormie Omartian recounts the story of one couple who called— right as dinner was ready—to say they couldn't make it. They'd just had an argument and didn't feel like they'd be good dinner guests. Stormie graciously urged them to come over, despite the argument. "You have to eat anyway, and if you have to, sit at opposite ends of the table." They ended up coming, laughing about the argument, and holding hands as they left. If we're wise enough to develop this kind of transparency, it can be transforming.

My husband once suffered a crushing disappointment. We were both incredibly disappointed and flirted with depression for several weeks. One of our male friends was exceedingly attentive to Greg during this time. He also worried about me because I was taking all this rather hard. I struggled with how to help Greg, and this man stayed close beside us. He called to check on me. He hugged me once. I began to notice endearing qualities about this man that I hadn't ever thought about. So I told my husband, "If I'm not careful, I'll develop a crush!" Voicing it out loud took the power away.

By the same token, one morning my husband casually told me about a scene in his office. A female student dropped by his office to chat and when she left, the two remaining students rolled their eyes and commented derisively about "her nerve."

"What nerve?" my sometimes naive husband asked.

"Are you *serious*, Mr. Dagnan? That girl has a severe crush on you! She's the president of your fan club!"

Although flattered, Greg confessed that while he noticed that a few girls seemed to find excuses to ask him about assignments, he hadn't thought too much about it. "I guess I just see myself as this middle-aged cop and professor whose duty belt fits a bit more snugly than it used to." I assured my husband that he was much, much more than that.

Not only did I appreciate my husband sharing this with me, but it reminded me that what we have is valuable and precious. I can't afford to take my husband for granted. One caution—don't overreact to such confidences or he won't feel comfortable sharing later.

My friend Vickie gently and skillfully monitors this aspect of her relationship with her husband too. She's married to a fireman; I'm married to a cop. We're aware that both professions have their groupies, and we've learned to be vigilant without smothering.

The truth is that infidelity doesn't necessarily develop out of a bankrupt system of moral values. Instead *personal values change to accommodate the affair.* What had been inconceivable prior to an affair can actually seem reasonable and even morally right after an affair. Many people who have always believed in being faithful in marriage find that their values do not protect them when they are faced with the temptation of an affair (emphasis mine).[5]

So how do these people stray so far from the truth? A few inches at a time. A rationalization one day. A brief feeling of euphoria that convinces them they're on the right track. Indulging in what seems like a tiny indiscretion.

If there is any surefire way to hurt me, it is to hurt one of my children. That's the very reason that Satan wants you. He wants me. He wants our marriages and our families because we are God's children.

Blurring the line in other areas of your life is a red flag smacking you in the face. Sexual freedom outside of marriage is, in reality, sexual bondage.

Accountability

Sometimes we don't need a friend who will tell us what we want to hear, especially in the vulnerable places of our marriage. Instead, we need someone brave enough to say, "What you are thinking about doing is wrong." Someone who will do all they have in their power to prevent our hearts from ruling our heads.

I do want to insert one extreme word of caution here. Never, never share your feelings of attraction with the object of your attraction! In fact, don't share those kinds of feelings with any member of the opposite sex. So many relationships may never have started if the parties involved had not unburdened their feelings in the wrong place. It's tempting to justify such sharing. *If we just get it out in the open, it will go away.* And we've just made Satan jump up and down in glee.

It is our nature to want to be adored, to feel protected. It is a man's nature to want to protect. When you share your marital hurts, that other man becomes your hero. *I would never treat you that way,* he assures. And we, in our tender vulnerability, fall for that hook, line, and sinker. We don't stop to consider how the hook will scar when it gets pulled out of our hearts, leaving a trail of bloody casualties behind.

Run, don't walk, to your nearest accountability group (aka your local church or Bible study group) to prayerfully and carefully seek out members. It would be fabulous if you could gently encourage your husbands to get involved in one too.

Choosing a Group

♥ Pray about it. (Beware of confiding in just anyone; sometimes the sympathy of a casual friend or coworker who has the "we all go through it" syndrome may have their own situations or agendas in which they don't wish to feel alone. Those attitudes may unknowingly push you toward divorce.)[6]

♥ Select same sex members who are strong believers in situations that parallel yours, perhaps adding a few who have been married longer to serve as mentors and as wise spiritual counsel. Older women "can train the younger women to love their husbands and children, to be self-controlled and pure, to be busy at home, to be kind, and to be subject to their husbands, so that no one will malign the word of God" (Titus 2:4-5).

♥ Make sure that there aren't too many members—small groups tend to grow intimate more quickly.

♥ Don't share too much, too soon. If these friends are new to you, build up trust with smaller issues. A proven friend will not be a gossip; they will guard information that you share with them.

♥ Institute a verbal or written contract assuring members that what is shared with the group stays there.

♥ Covenant to pray for one another. Keep a prayer journal so you can chronicle God's incredibly powerful answers through the years.

♥ There are several books that might prompt discussion of pertinent issues. One of them might be a great first meeting book and ease the transition into sharing more vulnerably.

Accountability Guidelines

Randy Alcorn's *The Purity Principle* offers some helpful guidance and questions that either lead to accountability or remind you where you might stand right now.

♥ Be active in a local Bible-believing, Christ-centered church.

♥ Surround yourself with friends who raise the moral bar, not lower it.

♥ Ask a mature Christian to mentor you as you walk in purity. *(Make sure this is a trusted member of the same sex.)*

♥ Join or form an accountability group. At every meeting, each person should answer these key questions:

  • How are you doing with God? With your mate? With your children?

  • What temptations are you facing? How are you dealing with them?

  • How has your thought life been this week?

  • Have you spent regular time in the Word and in prayer?

- With whom have you shared the gospel?

- Have you lied in any of your answers?

- How can we pray for you and help you?[7]

Boundaries

I am often asked, "Don't boundaries mean that I don't trust my husband?" Nope. If I have something that is truly special and valuable, I'm not going to leave it on my front porch hoping that someone won't come along and damage it or take it as their own. Don't trust yourself either; it is a lie from the pit of hell that infidelity could never happen to you. Remember that boundaries are loving and preventative actions, not suspicious mean-spirited afterthoughts.

Possible Boundaries

♥ Together, decide in advance what your boundaries are.

♥ Whenever possible, avoid sharing a meal or car rides with a member of the opposite sex. Both activities carry with them a certain degree of intimacy. During a necessary working lunch, keep the tone of all conversation at a professional level.

♥ When one of those activities is unavoidable or necessary, be in as public a place as possible and let your spouse know. At the airport after one of my speaking engagements, I ran into a minister I knew who had also been speaking. We were booked on the same flight home and there were several hours before departure. At the crowded restaurant we were seated at the same table. As soon as we placed our order, we got on our respective cell phones and let our spouses know. We also asked for a table at the front and in the open. It wasn't that we knew each other well or were particularly attracted to each other, but for the sake of our reputations, our witness, and our spouses, we removed all doubt.

♥ Make your own personal love story such a part of your life that you have instant recall of the feelings and images that made your love new. Watch your wedding video together on your anniversary.

Wear your wedding band. Talk about your husband and your family at work. Consider renewing your vows, at least to each other. Most of us don't think of doing this because we don't think we'll consider breaking them. Statistics make that a rather foolish thought.

♥ Make a personal plan for when, not if, you're ever attracted to someone other than your spouse. What same sex, trustworthy friend would you tell? Write down a list of consequences and people whom you would have to tell if you were unfaithful. One of our minister friends keeps just such a list in his top drawer at the church office. If nothing else works, fear can be a great motivator!

♥ Schedule a weekly date or a connecting time that is sacred. Write it on your calendar and make sure your husband places it on his too. When our girls were all very young, 9 to 10 p.m. was couple time. We didn't answer the phone, and soon even our friends were trained not to call at that time. Now that our oldest is a teenager, this time isn't as private. However, we've invented other things and will occasionally just tell her that she needs to be in her room.

♥ Avoid flirtatious conversation, even in a joking manner. I tend to be a very affectionate person who has the misfortune of being pretty naive. When we were first married, my husband, although not jealous in the least, helped me see that men might be responding to me differently than I had intended. I try to be more conscientious. If I've returned home from a speaking trip and think someone has flirted with me, I tell Greg about it. Sometimes he has insight into the flirtation triggers that I've overlooked.

♥ Be careful with your touches. I've even been known to ask permission from someone's spouse if something warrants a hug.

Jerry Jenkins makes a profound statement to those who might scoff at the need for boundaries: "No one thinks he needs hedges until it's too late."[8]

Sometimes boundaries need to include the removal of the source of a temptation. Scripture tells us to "resist the devil and he will flee from you" (James 4:7). It does not say "resist temptation and it will flee." In his book *The Purpose Driven Life,* author and minister Rick Warren reminds us that we have to refocus our attention and take action because thought resistance doesn't usually work. "It only intensifies our focus on the wrong thing and strengthens its allure." The more we tell ourselves not to think about what we can't have (even if it's just the too expensive sweater or the extra piece of chocolate cake), the more we desire it—crave it even.

Men who travel frequently for their jobs can be particularly vulnerable to visual temptations on cable or pay-per-view stations in the privacy of their hotel room. At a men's conference, Randy Alcorn once asked for tips for avoiding that sort of sexual temptation. One brave soul confessed that for years he had watched inappropriate movies in his hotel room. He would resolve each time that it would be the last. "After repeated failures he finally decided to do something drastic. Now when he checks into a hotel, he asks for the TV to be removed from his room. Although the staff may question him, he politely insists, and he has never been refused."[9] I don't even know this man, but I am so proud of him.

～

What courage and resolve it takes sometimes for us to literally flee. Remember Joseph from the Bible? If anyone deserved a beautiful woman, surely it was he. His jealous brothers thought about killing him, but instead sold him into slavery. Eventually he was noticed by Potiphar, the captain of Pharaoh's guard. Joseph became Potiphar's personal attendant and was placed in charge of his household. "So he [Potiphar] left in Joseph's care everything he had; with Joseph in charge, he did not concern himself with anything except the food he ate" (Genesis 39:6).

Can you imagine trusting a foreigner, a relative stranger so much that he has a key to your house, free rein in all that you own, and is privy to your finances? But our story doesn't end there, girlfriends. *Desperate Housewives* has nothing on the book of Genesis for intrigue, drama, and sexual pursuit!

"Now Joseph was well-built and handsome, and after a while his master's wife took notice of Joseph and said, 'Come to bed with me!'" (Apparently she was so brazen that she skipped over all the red flags, the flirting, and got right down to it!)

See Joseph's character: "But he refused. 'With me in charge,' he told her, 'my master does not concern himself with anything in the house; everything he owns he has entrusted to my care. No one is greater in this house than I am. My master has withheld nothing from me except you, because you are his wife. How then could I do such a wicked thing and sin against God?'" (Genesis 39:6-9). That's a lot of drama, huh?

Joseph does two significant things. First, he reasons with her, reminding her that he is in charge *because he is trusted* and that she is married. Second, he gets the sin exactly right—this sin is against God. Notice that he doesn't deny being attracted to her. I imagine that on a physical level, he probably was. He was a man. However, her tacky behavior, coupled with Joseph's character and the potential consequences, enable him to make a wise decision. Mrs. Potiphar is relentless!

"And though she spoke to Joseph day after day, he refused to go to bed with her or even be with her" (verse 10). Smart man. He went out of his way to avoid her. However, one day, she plots and plans and catches him alone. Literally. "She caught him by his cloak and said, 'Come to bed with me!'" (verse 12). But Joseph shrugged out of his cloak and ran. He wasn't even rewarded, at least immediately. The scorned Mrs. Potiphar told everyone that Joseph had tried to take advantage of her and used the cloak he left behind as evidence against him.

You might feel that way too. You might be going through a season of loneliness in your marriage that is so parched you feel desperate for someone's love. You may ache at the thought of switching jobs, moving departments, or giving up what you think is a harmless flirtation. Life will seem empty after that you think.

One precious lady came up to me after a marriage seminar and waited until everyone else had walked away. Her husband was so busy with work that he was all but ignoring her. She'd been going to a chiropractor each week. This man was single, handsome, and giving all the signals that he was attracted to her. She hadn't confirmed that this was a mutual attraction to him, but she recognized it in herself. What she wanted to ask me was if it was absolutely necessary that she stop going to this particular doctor. "I have an appointment in two days," she said as her eyes filled with lonely tears. Mine filled along with hers; she so longed for someone to love her. We prayed together, outlined a plan for talking to her husband, and she agreed to cancel her appointment. I knew it wouldn't be an easy battle because before exiting the room she turned back to me and asked, "What if he wants to know why I cancelled?"

The problem with flirting is that with a spark there's no way to contain the fire it might set off. Pairing one woman's gaping emotional need with a man's powerful sexual appetite is asking to burn down the whole house!

When the Spark Becomes a Flame

Contrast Joseph's story with that of King David, the man after God's own heart. Second to the story about David slaying Goliath is the story about David's famous fall recorded in 2 Samuel 11. "In the spring, at the time when kings go off to war, David sent Joab out with the king's men and the whole Israelite army...But David remained in Jerusalem" (verse 1).

Idle hands might not be the devil's workshop, but they're certainly fair game as his playground! "One evening David got up from his bed and walked around on the roof of the palace. From the roof he saw a woman bathing. The woman was very beautiful and David sent someone to find out about her" (verses 2-3).

And "after desire has conceived, it gives birth to sin," James 1:15 warns us. David allowed his desire to conceive a plan. "She came to him, and he slept with her...Then she went back home" (verse 4). In the very next verse we find out the consequences of a single night of passion and desire: "The woman conceived and sent word to David, saying, 'I am pregnant'" (verse 5).

We aren't given details. We don't know if the attraction was mutual for her, or perhaps she was afraid to say no to the king. Maybe it was as simple as not thinking it through—of making the age-old mistake of assuming that there can be such a thing as casual sex with no consequences.

If you're not familiar with the end of the story, David eventually called her husband, Uriah, back from the fighting to entice him to sleep with his wife (so the paternity wouldn't be questioned). But Uriah had such integrity that he refused to dine at home and to lie with his wife—even after King David got him drunk—out of loyalty to the men who remained in the difficult, uncomfortable conditions of battle.

Then David gave orders to send Uriah to the front lines of battle and withdraw the rest of the troops so he would die. Adultery. Conspiracy to commit murder. A child born out of wedlock. A pretty high price to pay for lusting on a rooftop.

David could have resisted the lust through prayer, accountability, taking a walk, a cold shower—but he didn't. Scripture leaves us such stories for a warning; even when we are very close to God, it is possible to stumble into sin. We can't let up on our diligence, even for a second.

Sexual Intimacy

Sex is an important indicator of the health and strength of the rest of your marriage. Sex involves unveiling our souls, ourselves, and oh yes, taking off our clothes! Gulp! Dr. Archibald Hart, in his marital research, concluded that "total openness in the arena of sexuality is the best protection I know against adultery." That's a pretty strong indicator of how important sex is in a relationship.

Allow your husband free access to your body whenever possible. Revisit the last chapter for fresh ideas to revitalize your love life and to remind the love of your life that you cherish him.

A Quick Memo to Husbands

"Most men don't realize, psychologically,
how vulnerable a naked woman can feel. The very act of
sex is one in which she is inviting someone else into her body.
You can't get any more intimate than that."

Dr. Kevin Leman in *Sheet Music*

~

Case Studies

Tina—discontent. Tina felt as though she had made one too many sacrifices when her husband decided to go back to college for a mid-life career change. An unexpected pregnancy further cemented her restless feelings of discontent. She began losing weight, buying new clothes, and wearing lots of makeup. One night she left her husband and five children to move in with a much younger college student. She ignored the phone calls and visits from her church friends who were urging her to go back and keep her promises. Later she ended up with another child by this man. She now works the perfume counter of a major department store.

Julie—disrespect. Julie looked at her husband with an increasingly critical eye. She hounded him because he had gained a bit of weight, had a boring job, and had not given her enough time with her friends. She started to flirt with an office colleague; the relationship turned physical more quickly than she could've imagined. Standing on her friend's doorstep, she admitted that her husband was faithful and a good husband, provider, and father, but she just wasn't in love with him anymore. She pushed through a divorce, alienating both of her sons in the process.

Rachel—insecurity. Rachel sentenced her husband to a lifetime of hard complaints...about herself. She was too fat, too boring, too lonely, too frumpy, too you name it. She expected her husband to silence the self-criticism with unreasonable expectations. She checked his email, monitored his phone calls, and dropped in on him at work. She lived in constant fear that he would leave her or have an affair. Sure enough, one day she was right. She told everyone who would listen about her mistreatment at the hands of the horrible monster her husband had become.

Johanna—isolation and loneliness. Johanna's husband was often on the road traveling for work. They didn't have children and she was often lonely. The computer in their home office beckoned and she struck up an online friendship with a charming, witty man who "listened" to all her problems and promised that life with him would be different. She believed him and agreed to an in-person meeting. She left her husband and married her Internet interest. She now regrets her decision and once again feels trapped.

Did you notice the common threads? Too much introspection. Shallow commitments. Chronic comparisons. Disrespect that led to seemingly insurmountable discontent. It's wise for us as women to be aware of some potentially dangerous times in our marriage.

Danger Points
While you don't want to take on a spirit of fear about your marriage, it is important to have your eyes open, especially during time periods when a relationship and individuals can be more vulnerable and at greater risk.

Big Transitions
A move, a major life change, the birth of a child, significant loss or

gain of income. Be especially aware of these challenges and increase your diligence in your marriage. Your accountability group is a lifeline during these times.

Teenage Years

The years when children become teens are reported to be those of highest marital dissatisfaction. Step up the date nights. Set clear boundaries with your teens and keep your relationship with your husband top priority. Answer questions and make discipline decisions as a united front. When I was in high school there was a couple whose college age sons often double-dated with them or my own parents! And really, a good time was had by all.

Midlife Crisis

Thirty-four is when the average mother sends her last child off to school. Thirty-five begins the average age of infidelity. Thirty-five is when the average married American woman reenters the working world. Thirty-four is the average age at which the divorced woman takes a new husband. Thirty-five is the most common age of the runaway wife.[10]

Instead of making it a crisis point, try to center yourself. By all means, try a new look, take up a new hobby, read outside your preferred genre, or take a class. Include your husband in your thoughts, plans, dreams, worries, and concerns.

Recommended Reading
The Second Half of Marriage, Dave and Claudia Arp

Beth Moore, in her practical, hard-hitting book *Praying God's Word*, points out that "Satan's attacks on sexuality have become so outright and blatant that we're becoming frighteningly desensitized and are unknowingly readjusting the plumb line to a state of relativity. In other words, instead of measuring our lives against the goal of Christlikeness, *we are beginning to subconsciously measure our lives against the world's depravity."*[11] (The emphasis is mine.)

Did you catch that? We find ourselves saying, at least in the confines of our minds, "What I'm doing/thinking isn't that bad compared to what everyone else is doing." Christian couples flirt with danger or outright embrace it. "God made me with these appetites." "There's no harm in just looking." "It's only a movie—it's not like we're actually inviting other couples into our bedroom."

Scripture reading and Scripture memory are both vital tools in constructing healthy marriage boundaries. Specific scriptures must be in our hearts so we can hurl them at Satan with promised success. Your commitment will matter to those around you, to your children, to those before whom you made that promise—count on it.

> *"Purity is always smart;*
> *impurity is always stupid."*
>
> RANDY ALCORN

The Aftermath

Without question, the most tragic consequence of divorce is what it does to our children. Several landmark studies, which have followed children of divorce, have found that in comparison to the rest of the population they have higher rates of depression, suicidal thoughts and attempts, health problems, childhood sexual abuse, school drop out, failure to attend college, arrests, addictions, teen pregnancy, and failure to keep jobs and relationships.

Even without such visible hurts, the insecurities and cracks are there. There is the myth of the "good divorce" (an amiable one) and certainly it is better than a bad one (hostile and combative), but it "does absolutely *nothing* to diminish the radical restructuring of the child's universe."[12] Divorce, because of its nature, asks children to keep secrets (attempting to prevent hurt to one or another of the parents), to surrender innocence, and forgo security.

The unity and security that a marriage provides are subtle, but vital to a child. They see their parents go into and come out of the same bedroom. They view these two separate people as a special plural unit—"my parents."[13]

To divide that unit is devastating to children. Their much-touted "resilience" isn't as resilient as we might selfishly hope. In contrast, children in two parent families generally have better academic achievement, less depression, and fewer serious behavior problems. This is even more true of parents who stay actively involved in their children's lives and build family memories.

Couples who ignore these facts are increasing in numbers. Sadly Christian marriage statistics are no better. One of my own relatives ditched her family to marry someone she met on the Internet! It was painful to hear her husband plead for her to honor her commitment and to know that she was deaf to those pleas. Not surprisingly, the children were the ones who suffered the most.

Marriage with a Mission

Every successful business and many churches have a mission statement. It keeps them on track. It is a clear, succinct, measurable, and understandable pattern for what you do and want to accomplish. It must be supported by all parties involved, upper level management all the way down to the janitors.

I strongly urge you to craft a mission statement with your husband; it can't really be done alone. And it has to be simple enough that if you told it to your children, they would understand. What questions need to be answered in a mission statement? Who are we? What do we do? Why do we do it? What do we value? Your mission statement will drive your marriage. It needs to be no more than two sentences because, as my husband tells people when they want his consulting help in developing a mission statement, "If you can't remember it, you can't live by it."

No matter how great it is, refuse to take your marriage for granted. Keep your vows, even when it's the hardest thing to do.

Chocolate-Covered Questions

1. What boundaries, if any, do we already have in place to guard our marriage from the fracture and pain of infidelity?

2. Are there ways we might anticipate temptation? What are your thoughts?

3. It is incredibly important that those in your accountability group be mature people of faith who are *trustworthy*. If you do not already have such a group or friend, list a few people that you think could be such partners. If you can't think of any, ask God specifically to bring someone like this into your life.

4. What are some current TV shows that depict immorality or sexually explicit situations? (As of this writing, I am thinking specifically of *Desperate Housewives*. We don't have cable but I'm *sure* there are others.) How do we know about those? If we now watch or are tempted to watch some of these shows, what could we do to change that habit?

5. One morning our minister posed this question about temptation and 1 Corinthians 10:13: "How many of you have had the way of escape and didn't take it?" He looked out over the crowd. "I see a lot of hands and a lot of dishonest people!" Has there been any situation you are willing to share in which you saw the way out but chose to ignore it?

   Covenant together as a couple to memorize that verse if you haven't already.

6. Proverbs 6:32 states that "a man who commits adultery lacks judgment; whoever does so destroys himself." If people know that's a lapse in judgment, in your opinion why don't they stop themselves?

7. How is it true that unfaithfulness destroys ourselves? What circumstances make us most tempted to let our guard down?

8. Read Proverbs 7:4-5. What two things do those verses say will keep you from adultery? _____ (your sister) and _____ (your kinsman).

SCRIPTURE

"Flee from sexual immorality. All other sins a man commits are outside his body, but he who sins sexually sins against his own body. Do you not know that your body is a temple of the Holy Spirit...? You are not your own; you were bought at a price. Therefore honor God with your body" (1 Corinthians 6:18-20).

HOT CHOCOLATE TOPIC

Are we keeping TABS on our marriage?
What's our weakest point? Our strongest?

GOODNIGHT KISS

Love of my life, I have been faithful to you today.

WHAT WOULD YOU DO ON A FIRST DATE THAT WAS TURNING SOUR?

I'd run home and play dead.
The next day I would call all the newspapers and make sure they wrote about me in all the dead columns.

CRAIG, AGE 9

Captivated by Chocolate

What You Love Most

My husband said he needed more space,
so I locked him outside.

Roseanne Barr

Inventor Alfred Nobel once woke up and read his own obituary in the paper (it was an error—his brother Emil had died). The article remembered him for amassing a fortune from his invention of dynamite. "He wanted to be remembered for something other than figuring out a way to kill huge numbers of people at once and making a lot of money doing so. So he initiated the Nobel Prize, saying, 'Every man ought to have the chance to correct his epitaph in midstream and write a new one.'"[1]

We probably won't have the unique opportunity given to Mr. Nobel, but we have the chance, no matter what stage our marriage is in, of reinventing our most prized relationship. We can make a conscious choice to treasure it. To appreciate it for what it is, not what we'd like it to be. We can become more grateful. We can infuse delight, joy, spontaneity, and new life into our marriages. Psychologists are discovering that people can change their behavior throughout their entire lives; we don't become stagnant at a certain age. Unless we choose to be.

I love the classic Mark Twain statement, "Most folks are about as happy as they make up their minds to be." And happy is something our husbands long to make us. Really. Sometimes we're just not very cooperative. We morph into the eighth dwarf, Mopey. Even though I am usually Tigger-like in energy and positive outlook (my daddy used to say that I have three speeds—fast, loud, and off), I do have my Eeyore moments. My husband invariably points this out to me if I let Tigger hibernate too long. "Where's my bouncy, positive Cinso?" he'll inquire with genuine concern.

Dr. Laura tells her callers that the cruelest thing you can do to your husband is to never be happy. Think about that. If he has a God-given instinct to protect you and a manly desire to fulfill you (think Tim-the-tool-man-Taylor howling "hoo, hoo, hoo!") and you're never responsive, never grateful, never positive, never happy, and never filled with wonder, you've condemned him to a life of misery!

The Wonder of It All

So what is wonder? Well, here are a few pretty wonder-full facts. According to experts, under normal conditions you can

- ♥ see a small candle flame from thirty miles away on a clear, dark night.
- ♥ smell one drop of perfume diffused through a three-room apartment.
- ♥ taste .04 ounce of table salt dissolved in 530 quarts of water. (Does this bring to mind *The Princess and the Pea* for anyone else?)
- ♥ distinguish between 300,000 different color variations.[2]

Amazing, right? So what about wonder in our marriage? Wonder was what I felt when I awakened during my first night as Mrs. Greg Dagnan and the moonlight gleamed in a soft path across my wedding band. Wonder is that God loved me enough to send His Son and then give me this gift of earthly love too.

I'll admit that it's hard to conjure up wonder once you've seen a man in his boxers and black dress socks, but it's an essential component of happy and committed marriages. It's an elusive quality than conjures up images of curiosity, mystery, intrigue, discovery, exploration, and contentment.

"Thus I have become in his eyes like one bringing contentment" (Song of Solomon 8:10). Do you hear the wonder in that statement? Is there any greater compliment you could receive from your husband than one in which he equates *you* with contentment? If that's one of your goals, then learn to view your relationship with eyes of wonder.

Don't let today be wasted by the desire to hold on to the past or concentrate exclusively on the future. Either direction ruins the myriad of chances each day holds. The weight of expectations lost or expectations disappointed can literally crush the life out of our marriages!

The basketball montage in *Father of the Bride* gets me every time! I was a die-hard daddy's girl and we have four precious girls of our own. Apparently it got to Dr. Neil Clark Warren too because after watching the movie, he made this observation. "to make peace with passing time, we must stay constantly alert, uncommonly focused, and as utterly present as possible at each moment. The only successful antidote for losing time is living and experiencing fully that time now, while it is the present."[3]

Here are some ways to experience wonder as a couple and as a family.

Pray Together

P-R-A-Y about specific goals you have outlined as a couple.

> **P**raise: Don't treat God as though He's stop number one on your neverending shopping trip. Praise Him for all He has done and will do. Thank Him for the gift of marriage and for understanding our need for companions. Thank Him for

the blessings of your children, your friends, your home, jobs, food, clothing, and various occasions for celebration.

Reflection and **R**emembrance: Mention to God where you are and where you would like to be in your marriage. Reflect on how your week and your day together has gone. Seek God's and your mate's forgiveness for any shortcomings. Bring up character qualities that you want Him to build in you. Remember specifically how God has answered your prayers and how He has held your marriage together in tough times.

Adoration and **A**sking: Adoration is a different facet than praise. It is naming the very character of God. It is announcing before Him who He is and what He is. Asking seems to come naturally in prayer, but perhaps you've never prayed very specifically. Go ahead. Although God knows what we need before we ask Him, we need to acknowledge our need *of* Him; to bow before Him and in our stillness, know that He is God.

Yearnings and **Y**ieldings: Share the deepest desires of your heart for your marriage. Surrender your potential, your hurts, your dreams, and your will to His. I won't kid you—it's the hardest prayer and the best prayer you can pray.

Serve Together

Although this is a model for community involvement suggested by Randy Frazee in his book *The Connecting Church,* it is easily adapted for families and couples.

Spiritual Formation: We will help each other grow.

Evangelism: We desire that our neighbors know Jesus Christ.

Recreation: We will have fun together.

Volunteerism: We will volunteer to help our church.

International Missions: We will help the church internationally.

Care: We will care for each other.

Extending Compassion: We will help the poor and needy in our community.

As young girls growing up, my sister and I went through the typical preteen and adolescent angst over the most ridiculous things. When we became too intensely introspective, we would on occasion complain about being down. "I'm depressed, Daddy," we would whine.

Daddy's chipper response, with our way-too-cooperative mother grinning in the background, was always, "Well, then quit thinking about yourself so much!"

I didn't appreciate it much at the time, but the older I get, the more it makes sense. Looking outward and taking the focus off of ourselves can be just the tonic we need. Even more, raising our children in the "nurture and admonition of the Lord," encouraging our spouse in his walk with the Lord, doing good "especially to those who belong to the household of faith," reaching out to proclaim the gospel in our neighborhoods and to our world are commands! In a nutshell, these are acts of service.

> **S**—Join a small group study as a couple, read Scripture together, take up a Christian devotional that you can do together. Institute and hold sacred a family night which includes devotions that can range from the simple to the spectacular! It can be reading a parable or watching a Veggie Tales video, and then talking about how to apply that Bible lesson to the people you know. Take along a dramatized version of the Bible on CD in your car, get ready in the morning to the sounds of praise and worship music, place your hands on each other or join hands in a family circle and pray for each other before you dash out the door in the mornings. In chapter ten of my book *Who Got Peanut Butter on My Daily*

Planner? there are fun, proven suggestions for family nights, daily rituals, and prayer times that develop and cement the spiritual dimension. There is no substitute for modeling time with God, individually and as a unit, for your children.

E—When we notice a new family has moved into our neighborhood, we take a small colorful gift sack, fill it with lemonade mix and cookies in spring and summer or brownie mix and packaged hot cocoa in fall and winter, a church bulletin, and a small card introducing ourselves and where we live. We walk it over to their home and hand it to them in person. It's a small thing, but we're hoping to teach our children about telling others about Jesus.

R—Make time for fun! Yes, do family things and special things with your children, but especially reserve something silly or fun just for you as a couple. Take ballroom dancing. Go to the theater and stay for two movies back to back! Go on a French fry date, grabbing a super-sized cola at the first stop and sampling all the fries along your fast food route. Camp out at least for an hour under the stars. Jump on the kids' trampoline. Take a midnight swim without your swim suits. Some of our good friends took an anniversary trip last year. They promised their kids that they would bring back pictures. Their youngest daughter was looking through them and noticed a hot tub in one photo. "Oh, Mommy," she said sadly, "you forgot your bathing suit—bummer for you!" That has become a hilarious catch phrase because their private quarters allowed them not to care one bit about swimming suits!

V—Participate in a church work day or volunteer to teach a Sunday school class for a season. Be youth group sponsors together. Or, if you have the talent, commandeer the church kitchen and prepare wonderful meals for church socials and banquets, like my good friends David and Sharris do. It is so neat to watch them serve this way together, and my home church is thankful that Greg and I have found other opportunities in which to serve!

I—This can be as simple as filling a shoe box for Operation Christmas Child or adopting a child as a family from Compassion International. When your children are older, go on a family or couples' mission trip. Right now our family has a "no Pop Tart week" (our children can learn about sacrifice). Each month we give the $5 we would have spent on Pop Tarts to a preacher's family in Cuba. We are humbled by their emails expressing how grateful they are for such a small thing.

C—Obviously, families who don't genuinely care about each other won't survive—couples won't either. Get actively involved in each other's lives and reach out to others too. You might combine a family night with another family from your neighborhood or church. Take time to ask them questions and actively listen to their childhood stories, funny experiences, work stress, and coping strategies. These folks are your future roommates in heaven.

E—As a couple or as a family, serve a meal at a local shelter. Take your family caroling around the neighborhood. Keep some fast-food certificates, inexpensive New Testaments, mittens, and umbrellas in your car for spontaneous distribution as you see various needs.

Parent Together

Read a Christian parenting book together. Pray for and with your children together. Consider beginning your week with a family prayer circle where all of you voice your needs for the coming week. Be sure to include time to praise God and mention what about each child you are most thankful for.

Love Together

It's unlikely that you will seek wonder if you don't plan on loving each other for the rest of your lives—that deep, mysterious wonder of "no matter what" love. A surgeon once wrote of this kind of love.

I stand by the bed where a young woman lies, her face post-operative, her mouth twisted in palsy, clownish. A tiny twig of the facial nerve, the one to the muscles of her mouth, has been severed. She will be thus from now on. The surgeon had followed with religious fervor the curve of her flesh; I promise you that. Nevertheless, to remove the tumor in her cheek, I had cut the little nerve.

Her young husband is in the room. He stands on the opposite side of the bed, and together they seem to dwell in the evening lamplight, isolated from me, private. Who are they, I ask myself, he and this wry-mouth I have made, who gaze at and touch each other so generously, greedily? The young woman speaks.

"Will my mouth always be like this?" she asks.

"Yes," I say, "it will. It is because the nerve was cut."

She nods and is silent. But the young man smiles.

"I like it," he says. "It is kind of cute."

All at once I know who he is. I understand, and I lower my gaze. One is not bold in an encounter with a god. Unmindful, he bends to kiss her crooked mouth, and I am so close I can see how he twists his own lips to accommodate to hers, to show her that their kiss still works. I remember that the gods appeared in ancient Greece as mortals, and I hold my breath and let the wonder in.[4]

Tears blur my eyes as I type that story. I wonder. I wonder if I would have such courage to cry private tears and keep a much altered or chronically ill spouse in the elevated position he would need and deserve? Would he love me still? It is worth contemplating, committing, and steeling ourselves for. We have promised no less.

"Place me like a seal over your heart, like a seal on your arm; for love is as strong as death, its jealousy unyielding as the grave. Many waters cannot quench love; rivers cannot wash it away. If one were to give all the wealth of his house for love, it would be utterly scorned" (Song of Solomon 8:6-7). Wonder indeed.

A Quick Word to Husbands

It isn't always the gift itself. To us it's what the gift represents: time, money, sacrifice, and the effort of noticing what we enjoy. Here's an example of wonder and then an example of "makes you wonder."

On one of our first Valentine's Days together, my husband purchased a three-in-one volume of romantic novels by one of my favorite authors. He put clues around the house, creating a scavenger hunt for me to find it. When I located the book, there was a coupon inside. It read, "This coupon good for re-enacting the love scene of your choice during a romantic get-away." At the end of the month, he contracted my parents to watch Eden for us, and we spent a night and a day away. I thanked him well and often remind him that anytime he wants to repeat this gift, it will be richly rewarded!

On their first Christmas together, my friend Sharris and her husband learned a valuable lesson about differences in gift giving. Sharris' family spent much time and thought selecting special gifts for each other; in David's family a gift for a particular occasion wasn't as important. When David got home from work on Christmas Eve and discovered that he was short a gift, he ran back out to the only place that was open—an all night truck stop. David bought Sharris a decorative bell. To her credit, Sharris didn't throw the bell at David. Instead, she placed it on a shelf as a reminder. Girls, we need to let our husbands know what we need. Guys, we need you to be a bit more observant and sensitive to those needs.

Now, this doesn't mean Greg always gets it right or that David hasn't presented gifts in the spirit of wonder to Sharris. What it does reveal is how different a moment, an event, or an exchange can be when a little wonder is sprinkled in.

When Wonder Wanes

The bottom line of any marriage is a willingness to hold fast to the pattern that God laid out and a strong commitment to go the distance, even in the tough, boring, or daily times. Oneness and wonder combine into an exceptional sense of "we-ness." We really are in this together.

One of the dangers of pop psychology is that we're told to be so in touch with our feelings and emotions that we no longer exercise any self-control. We act touchy, grumpy, irritated, gloomy, and disgusted whenever and wherever we want to. We rein it in a bit for strangers or acquaintances, but we feel way too free to let it all hang out. Perhaps we should stuff some back in!

Moods are pervasive and contagious. What is it that you want your family to catch? How often do you want your marriage to need an inoculation against you? Perpetual moodiness can kill wonder.

Speaking of moods, not more than 20 percent of your communication should be about complaints![5] For most women, how sensitive we are is distinctly related to hormones, and therefore moods. Try charting your cycle. Give your mate a head's up and ask him to be more tolerant during that time of the month. You too—try to be a little slower to take offense when your hormones are fluctuating.

Even after several years of marriage, couples may pull away from each other in unhealthy ways, leading parallel lives as little more than roommates or taking off bandages, causing sore, raw places to develop in their oneness.

When I was teaching abstinence classes in our local high schools (volunteering for our local Crisis Pregnancy Center), I created a unique visual illustration to show how it was impossible to have union with someone and remain the same person, unaffected by the experience. I placed lots of Elmer's school glue on two pieces of bright construction paper and pressed them together. After several minutes, I pulled the papers apart. At the places where glue joined them, the paper was soggy and sometimes the color from one sheet transferred to the other, or left small holes. No matter how I blotted, wiped, or tried to dry the papers, they were forever changed.

In a positive way, so it is with wonder. When two become one, the one-flesh equation results in wonder. It is not possible to live so intimately with someone and not experience wonder. We know each other's habits, breaking points, favorite TV shows, and silly snacks. We predict moods and can sometimes finish one another's sentences. We can't be torn apart after that and still remain the same.

There are certain signs that you're sliding out of Wonderland and toward roommate status:

- ♥ Your attitude becomes resigned, "Nothing will ever change; it will always be this way."

- ♥ You become apathetic about whether or not you and your husband are truly connecting at a soul level. While working on this book, my husband called me on the phone, laughing in what can only be described as a very "guy like" manner. He shared with me something he'd heard on a passing radio talk show and thought I might want to include it in the book. "Marriage starts with a prince kissing a princess and ends with a bald guy sitting across the dinner table from a fat lady." What a demonstration of cynical apathy at its worst.

- ♥ You're basically living parallel lives, occasionally meeting in the middle for sex.

- ♥ You've developed the Scarlett O'Hara Syndrome by putting off all important conversations and actions (she's my favorite character in one of my favorite films, but she stinks as a model for good wives!). "We'll talk/think/do something about that tomorrow." What to do?

Statistically, homecomings are among the most significant times in a marriage. As stated before, studies show that those first seven seconds make a difference, so make them good ones!

Ten quick things you can do to restore wonder

1. Save your best and most special news of the day just for him.

2. Be the first to wish your spouse success and do what you can to ensure it.

3. Make a list of the special things he does for you. Tie it up with ribbon and lay it on his plate.

4. Eat dinner alone together, looking into each other's eyes as you listen without interrupting.

5. Hold hands while you watch TV.

6. Don't interrupt—even once—when he's sharing about his day, a funny anecdote from work, or a heartfelt concern.

7. Plan to meet him somewhere and make sure you arrive first. Watch him as he comes in. View his interaction with others, his mannerisms, his appearance, and his special qualities like you've never seen them before. See him through another woman's eyes.

8. Learn to cook something he loves even though you don't especially care for it.

9. Make pancakes together in your jammies for a late night candlelit snack.

10. Put a love note in his lunch.

Recommended Reading:
Creative Counterpart, Linda Dillow

Deviate from your normal routine. Do the unexpected. One evening, my husband and I were driving separately to church, a consequence of schedules, not choice. "What's for dinner?" he had asked earlier on the phone.

"Meet you at the Taco Bell drive-through!"

Three noisy, hungry, grumpy children happened to be in my car. I ordered and went to the second window to pay. Suddenly my mischievous streak overtook me. I could do a small thing to shake things up and make a memory at the same time.

"How much is that guy's order in the car behind me?" I asked the gum-snapping teenaged cashier.

"Um, $3.45. Why?"

"Okay. I'd like to cover that."

Her bored look gave way to raised eyebrows. "You mean you want to *pay* for his order?"

"Yep." I handed over the money. "And one more thing...would you tell that guy I think he's hot?"

"Do you *know* him?"

I smiled mysteriously as the cashier motioned furiously for another gum-snapping ponytailed compatriot. "This lady bought that guy's dinner and she wants us to tell him she thinks he's *hot!*"

Mercifully, my girls were shocked into silence. I winked at the Taco Bell employees and drove off. Eden, my oldest, exhaled and exploded with laughter. "Mom! That lady thinks you're *crazy!* You *are* crazy! Why'd you do that anyway?"

"I love your daddy, girls. I just thought he could use a reminder."

I knew I'd hit pay dirt when we reached the church parking lot. My husband exited his car and all but swaggered to the building.

～

Deliberately seek occasions to restore wonder. One of my biggest temptations in marriage is to think back on a particular snapshot of a favorite time in our lives together and want to go back there. I spend untold wasted effort trying to preserve a still shot of what is meant to be a major, moving motion picture!

Such attempts invite stagnation. I have a tendency to recall the splendor of our dating days (and man, were they good!) with fondness and a sentimentality that is usually reserved for the dearly departed. You know what I mean. When someone dies, it seems like we gloss over their foibles, annoying habits, and times they forgot something important to us—we take away their humanness. They aren't just under a tombstone, they're up on a pedestal!

I sigh when recollecting the giddy rush of feelings whenever he called, the surprise visits, lunches out, and cuddling in movies. I wistfully wish for another night on the town seeing *Miss Saigon* at St. Louis' gorgeous Fox Theatre. I look at my souvenir Broadway ticket key chain and note that it's a bit tarnished and some of the writing is nearly illegible. I recall spontaneous trips to Branson and powdered sugar-coated, chocolate-icing-filled treats at Dunkin' Donuts. But unless I'm reminiscing with Greg, it has every chance of being taken as a criticism, a signal of my distinct unhappiness with the more mundane way that things are now.

Interestingly enough, Greg does not share my perspective on this obsession with the past *at all*. When I asked him if he still loved me as much as he did 12 years ago, he was genuinely puzzled. "No. I love you more! We've had babies and losses and moves and changes and discoveries together. It's way deeper than what we had starting out."

Wow. That's something to consider! Life at our house is anything but dull with four children, a home prone to springing ceiling leaks, a golden retriever that likes to chew through fence posts, a writer who brings a tablet with her as she observes family life, a warm circle of friends, a fabulous church family, a mom who lives in town, and a hunky professor/cop husband.

Nope, I can't really say that our life is boring, mundane, or even predictable. But I so often fail to appreciate what I have. I'm trying to bring myself back to my usual way of thinking. Life is so much more than an adventure. Life brings us each a certain number of days. Each one is a treasure to be savored, unwrapped, and discovered. Wake up today and go treasure mining. I can promise you that you won't go away empty-handed.

> *"Ah, love—you are my unutterable blessing...*
> *I am in full sunshine now."*
> ROBERT BROWNING

Make these truly the wonder years.

♥ Give your husband ten index cards. On five of them, have him write down his five favorite sexual positions or "favors." On the other five, have him write down his five favorite companionship activities. Often take out your "wonder" deck and let him draw one card. Have fun!

♥ Go ice skating or hold hands during the couples' skate at your local roller rink. (A return to the eighties, anyone?)

♥ Take a class together to learn something new.

♥ Watch the sunset together (or the sunrise, you miserable morning people!) every night that you can.

♥ Pay attention to what your husband says in passing. You might find out that he'd always wanted a certain comic book or game or toy as a child, but never received it. Look for it on eBay or in antique shops and surprise him with it.

♥ Choose to regard your husband with wonder. I was stunned during a recent family night, while munching on popcorn, and watching the home video of Emily's birth. Yes, she was (and is) beautiful. Yes, we were enamored with her, counting little toes and admiring the dark shock of hair. But what struck me was my face as I interacted with Greg in the birthing room and the following day as he pushed me out to the minivan in the requisite wheelchair. I was glowing! We had eyes only for each other. I listened to him raptly. We laughed often and touched one another constantly. I grant you that we had only been married for eleven months, but still, I was amazed at how I had allowed that adoring quality to wander. Wonder is an attitude—wear it well.

♥ Look for opportunities to create and preserve Memory Makers.

♥ Watch a romantic movie. Think he won't be interested in this one? Think again. Men and women who watched a romance experienced an increase of more than ten percent in their progesterone levels, a hormone responsible for a subconscious desire to get close.

♥ His classic book *Love Must Be Tough* is full of great principles for use in times of crisis, but I want to focus on one statement that Dr. Dobson wrote in a letter to his wife, Shirley, about their many years together. "Who else shares the memory of my youth during which the foundations of love were laid?" Who indeed. Each time you celebrate an anniversary or an achievement together (paying off a bill, the first time the baby sleeps through the night, your first getaway in too long), you've helped cement your relationship. Keep those reminders (remember the witness piles?) before you.

♥ Don't put off doing the special things and don't save your best for special occasions. Some of the smartest advice I ever received was what made me beg to use our income tax refund for our tenth anniversary trip. I figured we'd wait and have a bigger blow out on our fifteenth or our twentieth or... But an older gentleman listened to me ramble about my someday plans and stopped me. "If I had it to do over again, I wouldn't put anything off. Don't wait 'til you think it's a special enough occasion; every day you have is special and you never know when it will be your last." He spoke from experience.

♥ Haul out the good china tonight. Why is company better than family? Don't save that really great dress for a huge event. Go ahead and wear it. Splurge when you can; save when you must. But don't ever scrimp on love and laughter. Adopt the attitude Ronald Reagan had when he wrote to his beloved wife Nancy... because he married her, his was not just a Happy Valentine's Day, but a Valentine's *life!*

～

One of the lines that cracked me up in the movie *Beaches* was when Bette Middler's character, a rather egocentric performer, said to her friend, "That's enough about me. Let's talk about you! What did you think of me?" It's not all about you! It's okay. You can be sad for a minute and I'll wait right here on the page sympathizing with you.

We've gotten confused by the world's constant streaming scream of entitlement. "You deserve it!" "You are worth it!" "They owe you something!" We want to be millionaires, idols, survivors, and extremely madeover. In some ways, ancient Athens had nothing on us. We're a nation of god and goddess wannabes.

Still, there's good news. In a *Ladies' Home Journal* poll, 97 percent of women reported a resounding "Yes!" to the question, "Do you still think your husband is 'the one'?" This is good to know for those of us who've grown enough not to want to live in NeverNever Land (second star to the right and straight on 'til morning), but not so much that we still crave Wonder Land. It's not impossible; it just might be a little farther than you thought.

> *Drink water from your own cistern,*
> *Running water from your own well.*
> *Should your springs overflow in the streets,*
> *Your streams of water in the public squares?*
> *Let them be yours alone,*
> *Never to be shared with strangers.*
>
> *May your fountain be blessed,*
> *And may you rejoice in the wife of your youth.*
> *A loving doe, a graceful deer—*
> *May her breasts satisfy you always,*
> *May you ever be captivated by her love.*
>
> PROVERBS 5:15-19

Consider pairing up with an older couple, who is more mature in the faith and can help mentor you in your marriage. Chances are they've been down this road and others you will soon travel. There is often not only sage wisdom and prime example in such a mentoring match, but a sweet and mellow acceptance of one another which has come from having lived life longer than you. Elderwisdomcircle .org is a growing website staffed by volunteers, aged 60 to 103, who "share insights gleaned the hard way—from life itself."[6] Shoot, I'm impressed that people that age are navigating the Internet!

The blending and uniting of two wills, two interests, two souls into one flesh, one body, is a phenomenal mystery of divine proportions. Two, and yet one. The math may not add up, but the miracle of its truth is nothing short of a lovely and sacred privilege. We would do well never to lose this awe and wonder. The practiced habit of remembering translates into reliving that wonder in our everyday lives.

A farmer once came in from the pasture, his heavy work boots tracking in mud and clods of dirt all over his wife's freshly scrubbed floor.

A visiting friend commented, "Those boots sure do bring in the mud! How can you stand it? Isn't that aggravating?"

"Yes," the farmer's wife gently replied, "they bring in the mud, but they bring him in too."

She knew the magic of wonder.

Chocolate-Covered Questions

1. Dave and Claudia Arp state that "a marriage is either going forward or backward; standing still is not an option." Do you agree with that assessment?

2. Classify our marriage. Is it going forward or going backward? What makes you think this? In what ways?

3. Like the second chance given to Alfred Nobel, what area of your marriage do you most wish you could do over or reinvent?

4. How successful are you at living in the moment? How does that affect the state of your marriage?

5. What have you done lately to deliberately foster the element of wonder in your relationship?

6. Are you more prone to view your marriage as an "ordinary life" or as "paradise"?

Scripture

"For nothing is impossible with God" (Luke 1:37).

Hot Chocolate Topic

How would you define the word "captivated"?
When are you most captivated by our shared life?

Goodnight Kiss

I've written a list of the five things that captivate me the most about you. May I share it with you?

How would you make a marriage work?

*Tell your wife that she looks pretty,
even if she looks like a truck.*

Ricky, age 10

Chocolate Glue

A Made to Last Marriage

The only man I know who behaves sensibly is my tailor; he takes
my measures anew each time he sees me. The rest go on with
their old measurements and expect me to fit them.

GEORGE BERNARD SHAW

There's a catalog that we get in the mail, usually around Christmastime, named *Back to Basics Toys*. Greg and I enjoy looking at it together partly because there are things in there we remember having and playing with as children: Flexible Flyer wooden sleds, red Radio Flyer wagons, Lincoln Logs, a horse with springs, alphabet blocks, Colorforms, Slinkies. I love the newer versions of retro toys—play kitchens and doll beds. Greg prefers the racing cars—Evil Knievel and Erector sets.

This year was different though. In light of this book, I sat down with the catalog and instead of just looking at the toys and remembering the thrill of choosing my "wish list" for Santa, I contemplated what it was that made these toys classics. They are solidly built—made to last. The designs are fetching, but without rough edges. They are fun to play with, but each requires either meeting a challenge or channeling the imagination. These qualities keep them from getting buried in the back of the closet or in the bottom of the toy box. They were classics because they endured.

During the course of my studies in history, I was always the most taken with the myriad of personal stories about World War II. The classic legend of Dietrich Bonhoeffer is one of my favorites. As the Nazis began to take control of Germany, their evil reach included an attempt to control the church. Pastor Bonhoeffer defied orders and was active in resistance efforts, even participating in a plot to assassinate Hitler. When it failed, he was taken to a concentration camp where he was executed just days before the Allies came to the rescue.

He lamented about the doctrine of "cheap grace." He feared that Christians didn't want to experience trials, just all the thrills. I'm not sure he's wrong. It's doubtful that most of us will ever be called to martyrdom for the cause of Christ. However, every time we keep our word, renew our commitment, or determine to honor God with our marriage, we remember that grace had a cost—the life of God's Son. Sounds like expensive grace to me. See, we're always just one generation away from not knowing God. If we don't do what He says, including obeying Him in our marriages, our children won't do it either.

We need to be flexible. To offer tough love and real grace. To be willing to take stock at different stages and seasons of our marriage and adjust accordingly. An annual retreat is a wonderful tool for doing just that. Work at that mission statement from chapter nine. The bottom line on marital longevity is affirmation of commitment and holding fast to a "forever mentality."

"The day will happen," said John Ciardi, "whether or not you get up." So up and at 'em! This is the first day of the rest of your marriage!

～

Remember your commitment. Last year I turned 40. My mom, Greg, and the girls contributed gifts, decorations, and a favorite meal, including the best cake my mom makes. Everyone went around the table and presented me with their surprise. My mother went last. First I opened an envelope with 40 one-dollar bills; I laughed at her cleverness. But then Mom handed me a tiny box. I shook it, specu-lating, for I couldn't imagine what was in it. I untied the ribbon and peeled off the paper. I took off the lid and promptly burst into tears. Nestled on a bed of white cotton were the original white gold wedding bands that my daddy had first given to her. After squeezing the stuff-ing out of my mother, I placed those rings on my right hand. Every day I feel the breath of a promise on my left hand and the weight of a legacy on my right. It is a double reminder of all that I've been given and all that I've promised.

～

Rescue your passion. I'm not talking about sex here; it's already gotten plenty of coverage in previous chapters. What I'm talking about is intense, focused enthusiasm for each other—the adventure that is your marriage. Greet your husband with ardor. Gaze at him with longing. Deliberately choose him above all others. You're learn-ing the tools—now make the commitment.

～

Relive the memories, and add to them. There is a story that my sister and I just loved to hear my mother and daddy tell. When my daddy asked my mother to marry him, they had no idea where they would live. I mean none! They were blessed when a professional gambler (this was hilarious to us, since our father was a minister) needed someone to live in his secluded country home and care for his horses while he was away for a year. Rent free!

Like most newlyweds it never occurred to them to plan for the future, and so during the tail end of a snowstorm, which deposited a foot of snow, they eagerly awaited the delivery of—ta da—a brand new stereo, their very first purchase together! It was one of those monstrous cabinets with a radio, turntable, and special compartment to hold their record albums. I remember it being in our house as a child growing up. Each time we passed it, we marveled that our parents were once young enough to place so much value on music!

One anniversary our girls were snuggled between us as we watched our wedding video. When it was over they sighed happily and little Ellie piped up, "It's too bad Mimi and Boppa didn't have any children!" We explained that Aunt Annie and I *were* their kids. "Oh," she said. "I meant the young kind."

～

Greg and I share so many stories and experiences. He knows about the time I was preparing dinner and talking to him on the phone when I saw a snake in the house—he drove like a maniac to get home. He was the one who had to tell me that my daddy died. He remembers dancing with me to Garth Brooks singing *To Make You Feel My Love;* he also understands the significance. He's been with me when dreams beyond my wildest imaginings have come true. He's also held me and prayed aloud for me in the middle of the night. He's willing to do battle for me over things real and imagined in order to preserve our marriage.

Every day we are adding to that storehouse of memories. And if we ever have to surrender to that insidious nursing home life, I have no doubt we'll be having wheelchair races and adding to our memories.

～

Rejoice in what's right, rather than looking for what's wrong. You'll never be content if you're not content with what you have right now. How I have resisted such a statement. Like so many, I have been guilty of living life on hold. I'll be happy as soon as the car is paid off, as soon as we get a new kitchen table, as soon as the remodeling is done, as soon as everybody is potty trained, as soon as this crisis passes or that celebration is here. Guess what? There's always something. My husband is faithful, witty, tender, handsome, patient, committed, ambitious with integrity. He's a great father and grows in his faith every day. What more could I want? I have this day, this moment in which to revel. Small celebrations are all scattered around the daily things of life like a sprinkle of wildflowers; I only have to pick one.

～

Revel in the small things. Gratitude is a powerful thing. J. Paul Getty was one of the richest men in his day. He was worth more than four billion dollars. Although he could have purchased anything he desired, I'm not sure he got this gritty gratitude thing. The *Los Angeles Times* quoted from his autobiography on January 9, 1981.

> I have never been given to envy...save for the envy I feel toward those people who have the ability to make a marriage work and endure happily. It's an art I have never been able to master. My record: five marriages, five divorces. In short, five failures.[1]

Kindness is another basic building block. Author and professor of psychology Dr. John Gottman, in his book *Why Marriages Succeed or Fail,* observes, "For a marriage to last there must be at least five positive interactions for every negative one between partners." How's your ratio?

A precious lady in my Thursday morning Bible-study group told the story of a couple in their young ministry days who had been married 65 years. The wife always called her husband "O.D."

"Come on, O.D.! We're going to be late!" "O.D., where are you?" "I'm over here, O.D." They weren't his initials, so finally overcome by curiosity, Ruth questioned her about it. The woman laughed.

"Oh, some days it stands for Old Dear; other days for Old Devil. It just depends on the mood and whether he's irritating me or not. But for sure, it can't be taken the wrong way!" That precious gentleman always opened the door for his clever wife, and they were very much in love after all those years.

～

Revive your sense of teamwork. Our family is likely experiencing one of those miniature seasons of which my daddy would have said, "This is once in a lifetime." Our middle two girls, Emmy and Ellie, are on the same Upwards basketball team. It is their first year to play ball—ever—excepting games of H-O-R-S-E and quick inequitable pick-up games in the driveway.

Greg and I sit on the bleachers, beaming and cheering, admiring the way they look out for each other and celebrate one another's successes. A few times they've been in a position to pass to each other and one time it resulted in a basket. You'd have thought they were Olympic hopefuls! There's nothing quite like watching your children do something that brings you together.

This particular something has been a poignant reminder that although we've had some struggles, Greg and I are on the same team. We want to succeed in our marriage. We are endeavoring to parent children—productive young women who will one day choose someone for a life's mate who is crazy about them and even crazier about Jesus. We are trying to choose community involvement, friendships, and acts of service that reflect Christ. We long to make a difference and to finish our marriage more in love than we were at the beginning of it.

～

Reveal your plans for the future. Our society currently awards those who wear the badge of busy, but this hardly allows the sweet time needed for dreaming. I double dog dare you to break that trend.

I once read a lovely thought that was attributed to Steven Wright,

"Everywhere is walking distance if you have time." Lazy, delightful words drifted down like snowflakes when I contemplated that. Amble. Leisure. Stroll. Relax. Nap. Read. Quilt. Rest. Peace. You have the opportunity to break the busy cycle. To build an intentional legacy. To model rich living for your children and yes, someday your grandchildren. Be purposeful in your goals for tomorrow—the future begins right now.

Future is a sweet word because it is laced with hope. "And hope does not disappoint us," the Bible assures. Not if it is based on Jesus Christ. It is safe to walk into a future where He has been first.

～

Reaffirm your determination to go the distance. Dr. Dobson strongly defended forever marriages—that God-ordained, "one man and one woman for life" concept—as the cornerstone of society in a recent editorial for *Time* magazine.

> Traditional marriage is God's design for the family and is rooted in biblical truth. When that divine plan is implemented, children have the best opportunity to thrive. That's why public policy as it relates to families must be based not solely on the desires of adults but rather on the needs of the children and what is best for society at large.

> This is a lesson we should have learned from no-fault divorce. Because adults wanted to dissolve difficult marriages with few strings attached, reformers made it easier in the late 1960s to dissolve nuclear families. Though there are exceptions, the legacy of no-fault divorce is countless shattered lives within three generations, adversely affecting children's behavior, academic performance and mental and physical health. No-fault divorce reflected our selfish determination to do what was convenient for adults, and it has been, on balance, a disaster. [God's plan for families] is still the foundation *on which the well-being of future generations depends.*[2]

212 - Hot Chocolate FOR COUPLES

Jesus strongly and clearly stated this when the Pharisees were badgering Him about divorce. Can't you hear them? "Yuh, huh! We are too allowed to divorce! It's even in the law!" Jesus firmly refutes their arguments. "Moses permitted you to divorce your wives because your hearts were hard. But it was not this way from the beginning" (Matthew 19:8).

"I hate divorce," I can just hear God's voice thunder from the pages of Malachi 2:16. He doesn't hate those who are divorced, but it breaks His heart. Why? Because it wasn't the plan. Because it hurts everyone involved. It hurts the witnesses. It hurts the church. It hurts us. But, it especially hurts our children. As mentioned earlier in this book, except for rare cases of abuse or chronic unfaithfulness, divorce is *never* the best option. Never.

In *Christian Counter-Culture,* Reverend Dr. John R.W. Stott succinctly and accurately names divorce as "a divine concession to human weakness." As a generation, I think we lust after young love. We admire it. We lament it when we feel our honeymoon period, our just-starting-out, breathless-whenever-he-calls days are over. But I've determined lately that the most beautiful sight is not the bride and groom, hands clasped, sprinting up the aisle in anticipation of a honeymoon and happily ever after. Rather, it's the couple whose steps are slower, more halting, but oh, so in tune with each other. They've spent a lifetime mastering this one-fleshness. The hands that clasp each other are spotted with age, roughened with time, gnarled with experience and hard work.

One of my favorite series of books is the Mitford stories by Jan Karon. Uncle Billy is the town joke teller, a patient, simple man. He is married to Miss Rose, who suffers from schizophrenia. At times it mystifies the little town of Mitford how Uncle Billy can cheerfully tolerate, love, and stay with his wife. At one point, having witnessed some especially cruel behavior, Father Tim, the rector of Lord's Chapel, asks Uncle Billy his secret.

Uncle Billy's answer is priceless. "Well, I gave her my word, don't ya know." On so many levels, it is truly that simple. Not easy, but simple. Promises kept seem to surprise the world, but they shouldn't surprise any of us. We gave our word on a day that should stand above all others in our heart of hearts.

Doug Larson put it this way, "More marriages might survive if the partners realized that sometimes the better comes after the worse." I love to ask people if I can look at their wedding pictures and hear the story of their courtship. If they're in their golden years, I pester them with questions and ask for suggestions to achieve this goal. Folks are usually happy to oblige and the long-married couples often echo Larson's sentiment.

The longer we're married, the better it gets. Oh, we've had our share of problems, but if you stay with it, you'll find it's always sweeter on the other side. I believe them. I've seen it happen. I crave it for my own marriage. Marriage cannot succeed based on emotion. This kind of longevity love is an action word, a verb rather than a flimsy, mushy noun.

Researchers posed the question "What does love mean?" to a group of four- to eight-year-olds. One little girl, Rebecca, age eight, answered this way, "When my grandmother got arthritis, she couldn't bend over and paint her toenails anymore. So my grandfather does it for her all the time, even when his hands got arthritis too. That's love."[3] I agree.

Greg and I have a fiftieth wedding anniversary as our goal. Nothing short of it will do. We tell our children we know we are going to make it because we have no other options. We are stuck. And since we're stuck, we might as well make it as much fun as we can! This truth assures the children that we are committed to one another.

The poem entitled "A Love Like This" at the front of this book was written for my parents in 1998, a few months before Daddy died. I knew time was short, just not how short, and I wanted to do something to show them that I had noticed this remarkable legacy of commitment. I superimposed the words of the poem over a portrait of them on their first Christmas together and framed it quickly in the car on one of our many trips to St. Louis. They tearfully read it together. I saw their hands squeeze tightly. It set on their bedside table to keep watch over the last few weeks of their life together. Daddy died just 12 hours after the birth of our third daughter.

After his death, I expanded it into a short story. A love story. It first appeared in my third book, *The Lights of Home,* and illustrates beautifully the tenderness of "old" love. My parents did not have a perfect marriage; I don't know anyone who does. But what they *did* have was affection, appreciation, mutual admiration, and a bedrock commitment to hang on no matter what. It's a commitment that is frequently absent these days. It's one that we need to return to, to live up to, and to leave as a powerful statement to our children and our children's children.

～

It began in a small rural town. A friendship spawned in a one-room schoolhouse. They were sixth graders. She was rail thin, awkward, and shy. He was tall, gangly, and athletic. He was the new kid on the square. She thought he was handsome. He thought she had the prettiest hair he'd ever seen.

But of course they weren't about to tell each other. So they engaged in all the typical behaviors of first affection. Hair pulling. Shin kicking. Name calling.

The town grew with their friendship. She typed his high school papers. He helped out with frogs in science. She cheered his basketball prowess. He admired her acting ability on stage. She collected the class rings of other boys (three, to be exact), trying to get his attention. He pretended not to notice and informed her that he wouldn't marry her if she were the last woman on earth!

My how things change. During their senior year they were cast as husband and wife in the school play. The final scene required a kiss—later they both agreed that it was intriguing.

They graduated and went away to college. He dated other girls, wanting to test the realness of this friendship with the possibility of real love. She cried into her pillow, thinking he didn't care. She got engaged to someone else. He took notice and asked her to call it off. She did.

A few months later, on a dimly lit dirt lane back in their hometown, he took the hand of the girl he'd loved since sixth grade. He slipped a diamond solitaire on her finger, all the while warning her about his intent to be a minister. There'd be hard times he predicted. Sacrifices of material possessions, of his time with her. She smiled and said she didn't mind.

So they married and he preached and served and wrote a column for the sports page of another small town paper. They had a baby girl and life was good. Another move, another town, and another baby girl was born. They planted a new church with four families and God in their midst. It grew to a church of 500. People wanted to see what difference God made in real life, and they saw it in this man who lived every day like it was a gift.

But one day the man was diagnosed with cancer. "It will go swiftly. Ultimately it will cost you your life," the doctor warned. But the doctor made such predictions without knowing the power of faith, of prayers that interceded on the man's behalf.

And the love of this man and his wife grew, bound up in a million different memories, cemented with the glue of commitment. They did not take lightly this promise they'd made.

The little girls grew up watching this example and claimed it as a pattern for their own someday loves. Before it seemed time, they left home, finished college, and married, blessing their parents with grandchildren.

Meanwhile, radiation and chemotherapy took their toll. The girls observed that their daddy loved their mother through the changes that time and childbearing had wrought. Their mother loved their father back, even when chemotherapy made his hair fall out and when it grew back, as soft and downy as a baby duck's.

Not many people have a love like this, the girls thought.

The miraculous gift of years passed, each day unwrapped with joyous anticipation, for all days given are presents. And one day the doctor gathered the family to tell them that the miracles were coming to an end.

The man told the doctor that God had been good to him. He hated to say goodbye, but when the time came, he would be ready to take the best seat in all the universe. The one where he would be glancing down between the stars, waiting for his bride and his girls to meet him there.

This is what love is. A love that stands when all else has fallen. It stands when a godly man leaves life at 56-years-young. It was faithful for thirty-four years, six months, eleven days, eight hours, and seventeen minutes. It's what we all want. It's what we need to be reminded of on our worst days. It is a love like this.

～

Did it make a difference, this commitment? To my sister and me, yes. To my children, yes. But I wondered if this had a larger impact, a wider reach that could inspire others. I found out at least some of my answer in a way that only God could have orchestrated.

Nine months after Daddy's death, I had a speaking engagement in St. Louis. Since I had not been able to be with my daddy when he died (we arrived for the visitation and funeral with my three-day-old infant, as soon as we were cleared to travel), I had a burning desire to see that hospital room. I drove straight there when I was done speaking. Because of new security measures, I had to sign in the name of the patient I was visiting. Flustered, I couldn't think and so I just wrote down Daddy's name, Don Sigler, the way I had done so many times before.

My eyes were already full as I stood beside the nurse's station. The first nurse who saw me was an answer to prayer. I explained my request in between great, gulping sobs. She told me there was a patient in that room, but that it would be all right if I wanted to stand in the doorway for a moment. She led me there, and I literally held my breath to keep from breaking apart or letting my pain escape in raw, noisy bursts.

I felt God's hands hold me then. Oh, my heart wasn't any less raw, but I knew, as sure as I'm typing this, that He is real and that He cares. He cares so much.

I looked at the bed. I imagined the scene. I remembered the last time I got to talk to him—my mother held the phone up to his ear so I could tell him of Baby Ellie's arrival and that I loved him so very much.

"Praise God!" Daddy said. "The baby's here and Cindy is okay. I'm ready to go home; take me now." But for the next 12 hours my father endured excruciating, unbearable pain. The whys haunted me.

In the video of my mind, I saw my always faithful mother sitting beside him, soothing him with cold cloths, getting him fresh sheets when the pain broke out as cold sweats all over his body. I heard them whisper together and reminisce. Occasionally I could see the watchdog part of my mom thrust her head in the hall and demand some relief for the love of her life. I squeezed my eyes tightly, not wanting to see that last moment when breath stole from his earthly body and the promises they had made were fulfilled.

The nurse came beside me in the doorway and took my hands in hers. "Sweetheart, what was your daddy's name?"

I told her.

"Oh, I remember him!" Her eyes lit up. "It was unforgettable. What your dad craved most was cold Coca Cola!" I interrupted her remembering with unladylike, snotty laughter.

"He was always so kind, telling us thank you. Sometimes it seemed like his eyes were shining and he had to have been hurting so bad. There were several people outside the door praying for him, but he spent most of his time talking to your mother and telling her how much he loved her and you girls. I was here when you called him about the baby. It was remarkable. He made such an impression on us and I know I'll never forget him."

I left the hospital for the last time knowing I had been given an incredible gift; I knew for certain that the legacy I had so idolized and admired had been sweet and true.

This is the prayer I have prayed for you, precious readers, since I first began this book's journey. I want us all to have a love like this. If marriage is a race, it is definitely a marathon, not a sprint. May your finish line surpass any sweetness you could have ever dreamed, and your reward exceed any you could have imagined.

CHOCOLATE-COVERED QUESTIONS

1. When filling out these planning sheets keep in mind that goals must be specific, measurable, and have a progression of steps along the way to fulfillment.

Examples:

Personal Goal #1: Lose ten pounds. Weigh in every Friday. Steps: cut back to single portions, up water intake, do aerobic exercise a minimum of three times per week for 30 minutes, do 20 minutes lifting free weights two times per week, have dessert only twice a week.

Spiritual Goal #1 : Memorize one new scripture verse every week. Write or recite from memory each Saturday. Steps: get accountability partner, select target verses, write or type verses on index cards, tape copies to mirror, steering wheel, and above kitchen sink.

Financial Goal #1: Pay off credit card. Balance must be smaller with no new purchases on every month's statement. Steps: make list of everything we spend money on every day for one month, cut back on visits to Starbucks, make no charge purchases without a) checking with each other and b) assurance that the purchase can be paid off at the end of the month, organize items to sell in garage sale and apply proceeds to card.

Marriage Goal #1: Institute and carry out a monthly date night. Success measured by whether or not we actually go. Steps: reserve time and place date on calendar, arrange childcare swap with another couple, list activities which we would enjoy doing on our dates, budget for our couple entertainment.

Relationships Goal #1: Spend more time with friends. Making a monthly commitment to a common activity. Steps: poll friends for interests (book club? Bible study? scrapbook club), organize details and delegate, put date on calendar, have fun!

Children Goal #1: To begin a fun one-on-one devotional study with each child. Begin by shooting for a target goal of twice a month per child. Steps: Take each child with me to Bible bookstore or browse through the resources in our home to solicit interest in specific age-appropriate books—make it fun, decide with each child what time frame would work best with them (before bed, after school, a weekend afternoon), and pray about this with and for my child, commit to this and ask spouse or accountability partner to check in with me, engage child in feedback.

Annual Goals Sheet					
Personal	Spiritual	Financial	Marriage	Relationships	Children

5-Year Plan Goals Sheet					
Personal	Spiritual	Financial	Marriage	Relationships	Children

10-Year Plan Goals Sheet					
Personal	Spiritual	Financial	Marriage	Relationships	Children

2. What "classic" elements, like those in the classic toys, does your marriage enjoy?

3. Of the two of you, who is better at looking at the positive elements of your relationship rather than dwelling on the negative aspects?

4. Do you agree that our generation and our society "lusts after young love"?

5. What are the benefits of "old love"?

6. Together read the poem "A Love Like This." What legacy story are you leaving for your children and grandchildren?

SCRIPTURE

"Enjoy life with the wife, whom you love" (Ecclesiastes 9:9).

HOT CHOCOLATE TOPIC

What single factor in our marriage do you feel serves as our chocolate "glue"? Is that factor the same as what you think it should be?

GOODNIGHT KISSES

Babe, they're playing our song. Let's dance. Slow dance. Right now, and anytime we hear it for the rest of our lives. Let's dream together about our next ten years!

"A husband who hadn't given his wife an anniversary present in years was feeling sentimental on the eve of their 25th anniversary. He asked, 'Darling, what kind of flower do you like best?' 'After 25 years,' snapped his wife, 'you ought to know it's Pillsbury!'"

—FOUND IN MY DADDY'S SERMON NOTES

Conversation Starters
for Married Couples

~

If you were president of the United States, what would be your top three goals?

What event in history do you most remember?

Who most influenced the way you are as a husband? As a father?

What dream have you never told anyone about?

What do you truly love or hate about your job?

What's the best thing about living with me? What's the worst?

If you were making a timeline of your life, what ten highlights would you show me?

What's the best thing we could do to transform our family schedule?

Abiding by the scriptural guidelines in chapter 8, do you have a fantasy, new location, or ??? that you'd like us to try?

What activity would you'd like us to do together?...Besides that!

If you could keep only one memory from childhood, what would it be?

If you could keep one memory from year of our marriage, what would they be?

When is it the hardest for you to pray? Why?

What do I do that makes it easiest for you to talk to me? What makes it most difficult?

If money were no object, where and in what style of house would you have us retire?

What color was your day?

If you suddenly inherited $500,000, what would you do with it first? After me, who would you tell about it first?

Pick five adjectives to describe our sex life.

What do you remember most fondly about our children's births?

Who was your favorite teacher? Why?

What is your favorite verse of Scripture? Parable? Who is your favorite Old Testament hero? Disciple?

If our house was on fire and you had time to save only one possession, what would you choose? (Note: The family is safe.)

Hot Chocolate Surveys

~

These are the surveys that were distributed at various collection points and by mail. Each participant was given the opportunity to place their answers in double envelopes. Incoming surveys were opened and sorted in groups of 25 to 50 so that anonymity could be preserved. Completing these surveys and discussing them can be a great exercise to do with your spouse, provided the following guidelines are set.

- ♥ Do this individually first.

- ♥ Think about what your spouse's answers might be.

- ♥ Discuss your surveys on an evening when peace reigns and you have unhurried time together.

- ♥ Pray about them before sharing.

- ♥ Be honest, but when explaining your answers to your spouse, be sensitive. Don't accuse, name call, or be defensive.

- ♥ Agree in advance that there won't be negative repercussions for honest answers.

Hot Chocolate Female Survey

1. Age _____

2. How many years have you been married? _____

3. Which is more important to you, *respect* or *relationship?*

4. Please rank the following in order of importance to you (1 being the most important; 8 the least important):

_____ respect

_____ feeling appreciated for your contributions to the household _____companionship

_____time with friends

_____sex

_____time alone

_____romance

_____love

5. What one thing would you change about your sex life? What do you think your husband's answer would be? Would you change the level of frequency or variety?

6. What does romance look like to you?

7. In what activities do you wish your husband would participate with you? (recreational, etc.)

8. Do you and your husband have an annual getaway time in which you take stock of your marriage, dream, and set goals together?

9. What is your current level of marital satisfaction? (10 is the highest, circle one)

    1 2 3 4 5 6 7 8 9 10

10. Why?

11. What factor(s) *inhibit* emotional intimacy in your marriage?

    Physical intimacy?

12. What factor(s) *encourage* emotional intimacy in your marriage?

    Physical intimacy?

13. What is the one thing you'd say you are most seeking from your husband?

14. How has your past or your husband's past (background, upbringing, previous marriages) affected your marriage?

15. What is your best tool for communicating clearly with your spouse?

16. What is your best piece of advice for couples?

Hot Chocolate Male Survey

1. Age _____

2. How many years have you been married? _____

3. Which is more important to you, *respect* or *relationship*?

4. Please rank the following in order of importance to you (1 being the most important; 8 the least important):

    ____ respect

    ____ feeling appreciated for your contributions to the household

    ____ companionship

    ____ time with friends

    ____ sex

    ____ time alone

    ____ romance

    ____ love

5. What one thing would you change about your sex life? What do you think your wife's answer would be? Would you change the level of frequency or variety?

6. What does romance look like to you?

7. In what activities do you wish your wife would participate with you? (recreational, etc.)

8. Do you and your wife have an annual getaway time in which you take stock of your marriage, dream, and set goals together?

9. What is your current level of marital satisfaction? (10 is the highest, circle one)

     1 2 3 4 5 6 7 8 9 10

10. Why?

11. What factor(s) *inhibit* emotional intimacy in your marriage?

     Physical intimacy?

12. What factor(s) *encourage* emotional intimacy in your marriage?

     Physical intimacy?

13. What is the one thing you'd say you are most seeking from your wife?

14. How has your past or your wife's past (background, upbringing, previous marriages) affected your marriage?

15. What is your best tool for communicating clearly with your spouse?

16. What is your best piece of advice for couples?

Survey Results
(75 representative samples)

Male Surveys

1. Average age: 40.8

2. Average number of years married: 13.9

3. 53 percent ranked respect as more important than relationship, 39 percent ranked relationship as more important than respect, 7 percent did not answer that question.

4. The average rankings for each of the eight qualities in order from most to least important:

     1. Love
     2. Companionship

   3. Respect
   4. Sex
   5. Romance
   6. Appreciation for their contributions
   7. Time with friends
   8. Time alone

5. Average level of marital satisfaction: 8.55

Note: Husbands generally were happier and more upbeat about their marriages than were wives.

Female Surveys

1. Average age: 42.3

2. Average number of years married: 16.4

3. 58 percent ranked respect as more important than relationship, 29 percent ranked relationship as more important than respect,* 23 percent did not answer than question.

4. The average rankings for each of the eight qualities in order from most to least important:

   1. Respect
   2. Love
   3. Companionship
   4. Romance
   5. Feeling appreciated for their role
   6. Sex
   7. Time alone
   8. Time with friends

5. Average level of marital satisfaction: 7.9

* Although the women rated respect as most important, their definitions from anecdotal comments seem to be vastly different than male definitions of respect. In fact, some answers seemed to confuse or equate with appreciation and romantic gestures. Males typically defined respect as performance based on the position as head of household, provider, etc.

Notes

~

Chapter 1

1. Alex Ayres, ed., *The Wit and Wisdom of Abraham Lincoln* (New York: Meridian, 1992), p. 124.
2. Alex McFarland, "30 Going on 18," *Focus on the Family,* February, 2007.
3. Elizabeth Marquardt, *Between Two Worlds: The Inner Lives of Children of Divorce* (New York: Crown Publishing, 2005), p. 187.
4. Beth Moore, *Praying God's Word* (Nashville: Broadman and Holman, 2000), p. 91.
5. Kevin Leman, *Sex Begins in the Kitchen* (Grand Rapids, MI: Revell, 1999), p. 41.
6. Paul and Sandy Coughlin, *Married but Not Engaged* (Minneapolis: Bethany House Publishers, 2006), p. 79.
7. Brent Curtis and John Eldredge, *The Sacred Romance* (Nashville: Thomas Nelson, 1997), p. 3.
8. Susan Alexander Yates, *A House Full of Friends: How to Like the Ones You Love* (Colorado Springs: Focus on the Family, 1995), p. 80.
9. Nancy Cobb and Connie Grigsby, *The Best Thing I Ever Did for My Marriage* (Sisters, OR: Multnomah Publishers, 2003), pp. 125-27.

Chapter 2

1. Gary Chapman, *The Four Seasons of Marriage* (Wheaton, IL: Tyndale, 2005) pp. 23-54.
2. Charles Swindoll, *Strike the Original Match* (Sisters, OR: Multnomah Publishers, 1980), p. 10.
3. Kevin Leman, *Making Sense of the Men in Your Life* (Nashville: Thomas Nelson, 2000), p. 123.
4. James Dobson, *Love for a Lifetime* (Sisters, OR: Multnomah Publishers, 1987), p. 65.
5. Larry Halter, Ph.D., *Traits of a Happy Couple* (Waco, TX: Word Publishing, 1988), p. 214.
6. Charlie Shedd, *Letters to Karen* (Nashville: Abingdon Press, 1965), p. 77.

Chapter 3

1. Charlie Shedd, *Letters to Karen* (Nashville: Abingdon Press, 1965), p. 45.
2. Quoted in John Eldredge, *Wild at Heart Field Manual* (Nashville: Thomas Nelson, 2002), p. 104.
3. Ed Young, *The 10 Commandments of Marriage* (Chicago: Moody, 2003).
4. Kevin Leman, *Sex Begins in the Kitchen* (Grand Rapids: Revell, 1999), p. 129.
5. Dr. Emerson Eggerichs, *Love and Respect* (Nashville: Thomas Nelson, 2004), p. 43.

6. Ibid., 42.

7. Ibid., 44.

8. Linda Dillow, *Creative Counterpart* (Nashville: Thomas Nelson, 1986), p. 122.

9. Leman, *Sex Begins in the Kitchen,* p. 244.

10. John Gray, *Men Are from Mars, Women Are from Venus* (New York: HarperCollins, 1992), p. 27.

Chapter 4

1. Dr. Laura Schlessinger, *The Proper Care and Feeding of Husbands* (New York: HarperCollins, 2003), p. 93.

2. John Gottman, *Why Marriages Succeed or Fail* (New York: Simon and Schuster, 1994), pp. 143-47.

3. Michael Gurian, *The Wonder of Boys* (New York: Tarcher, 2006), pp. 21-22.

4. Dr. Emerson Eggerichs, *Love and Respect* (Nashville: Thomas Nelson, 2004), p. 118.

5. Ibid, p. 70.

6. Scott Halzman, *The Secrets of Happily Married Men: Eight Ways to win Your Wife's Heart Forever* (San Francisco: Jossey Bass, 2006), p. 145.

7. These five levels of communication have been found many places. I chose to use the wording of the levels from John Powell's *Why I Am I Afraid to Tell You Who I Really Am?* in Kevin Leman's *Sex Begins in the Kitchen,* pp. 122-25.

8. *Ladies' Home Journal,* November 2006, p. 101.

9. Karol Ladd, *The Power of a Positive Wife* (West Monroe, LA: Howard, 2003), p. 222-23.

10. *Redbook* magazine, November 1999, p. 104.

11. Dr. Les Parrott and Dr. Leslie Parrott, *Questions Couples Ask* (Grand Rapids, MI: Zondervan, 1996), p. 37.

12. Dr. Susan Heitler, "Can This Marriage Be Saved?" *Ladies' Home Journal,* September 2006, p. 128.

Chapter 5

1. Cindy Sigler Dagnan, *Who Got Peanut Butter on My Daily Planner?* (Eugene, OR: Harvest House, 2006), p. 188.

2. Randy Frazee, *Making Room for Life* (Grand Rapids: Zondervan, 2003).

3. Ibid., p. 115.

4. Dr. Les Parrott and Dr. Leslie Parrott, *The Time-Starved Marriage* (Grand Rapids, MI: Zondervan, 2006), p. 35.

5. Alex Ayres, ed., *The Wit and Wisdom of Abraham Lincoln* (New York: Meridian, 1992), pp. 122-23.

6. Gary Chapman, *The Four Seasons of Marriage* (Wheaton, IL: Tyndale, 2005), p. 122.

7. Susan Alexander Yates, *A House Full of Friends: How to Like the Ones You Love* (Colorado Springs: Focus on the Family, 1995), pp. 75-77.

8. Dave and Claudia Arp, *The Second Half of Marriage* (Grand Rapids, MI: Harper Collins/Zondervan, 1996), p. 182.

Chapter 6

1. Dr. Laura Schlessinger, *The Proper Care and Feeding of Husbands* (New York: HarperCollins, 2004), p. 105.

2. Jill Savage, *Is There Really Sex After Kids?* (Grand Rapids, MI: Zondervan, 2003), p. 113.

3. Joseph Dillow, *Solomon on Sex* (Nashville: Thomas Nelson, 1977), p. 65.

4. Adapted from Henry Virkler, *Speaking Your Mind Without Stepping on Toes*, in Ellen Banks Elwell, *The Christian Mom's Idea Book*, (Wheaton, IL: Crossway Books, 1997), p. 79.

5. Elisa Morgan and Carol Kuykendall, *Children Change a Marriage* (Grand Rapids, MI: Zondervan, 2002), pp. 46-47.

6. Gary Chapman, *The Five Love Languages* (Chicago: Northfield Publishing, 1995), p. 48.

Chapter 7

1. Dave Meurer, *Daze of Our Wives* (Minneapolis: Bethany House, 2000), pp. 69-70.

2. Sheila Wray Gregoire, *Honey, I Don't Have a Headache Tonight* (Grand Rapids, MI: Kregel Publications, 2004), p. 23.

3. Dr. Joseph and Linda Dillow and Dr. Peter and Lorraine Pintus, *Intimacy Ignited* (Colorado Springs: NavPress, 2005), p. 161.

4. Paul and Sandy Coughlin, *Married but Not Engaged* (Minneapolis: Bethany House, 2006), p. 117.

5. Lois Walker, *Exploring*, in Kathryn Falk, *How to Write a Romance* (New York: Signet Books, 1989), p. 130.

Chapter 8

1. Kevin Leman, *Making Sense of the Men in Your Life* (Nashville: Thomas Nelson, 2000), p. 148.

2. Karen Scalf Linamen, *Pillow Talk* (Grand Rapids, MI: Revell, 1996), p. 189.

3. Wendy Shalit, *Return to Modesty* (New York: Free Press, 1999), p. 55.

4. Linda Dillow and Lorraine Pintus, *Intimate Issues* (Colorado Springs: Waterbrook Press, 1999), pp. 199-201.

5. David Zinczenko, *Men, Love and Sex* (New York: Rodale Press, 2006), p. 22.

Chapter 9

1. Dr. Les Parrott and Dr. Leslie Parrott, *Questions Couples Ask* (Grand Rapids, MI: Zondervan, 1996), p. 121.

2. Beth Moore, *When Godly People Do Ungodly Things* (Nashville: Broadman and Holman, 2002), p. 166.

3. Kevin Leman, *Making Sense of the Men in Your Life* (Nashville: Thomas Nelson, 2000), pp. 6-7.

4. Dennis and Barbara Rainey, *Staying Close* (Nashville: Thomas Nelson, 1989), p. 90.

5. Willard Harley, *Surviving an Affair*, in Sally Marcey, *Desperate House Lies*, (Sisters, OR: Multnomah, 2006), p. 13.

6. Diane Medved, *The Case Against Divorce* (New York: Ivy Books, 1990), p. 75.

7. Randy Alcorn, *The Purity Principle*, in *MasterWorks* (Nashville: Lifeway Press, 2006), p. 36.

8. Jerry B. Jenkins, *Loving Your Marriage Enough to Protect It* (Chicago: Moody Press, 1993), p. 13.

9. Ibid., p.50.

10. Gail Sheehy, *Passages* (New York: Dutton, 1976), pp. 378-83.

11. Beth Moore, *Praying God's Word* (Nashville: Broadman and Holman, 2000), p. 273.

12. Elizabeth Marquardt, *Between Two Worlds: The Inner Lives of Children of Divorce* (New York: Crown Publishing, 2005), p. 16.

13. Ibid., pp. 22-26.

Chapter 10

1. Nancy Cobb and Connie Grigsby, *The Best Thing I Ever Did for My Marriage* (Sisters, OR: Multnomah Publishers, 2003), p. 28.

2. *Family Circle,* July 18, 1995, p. 52.

3. Neil Clark Warren, *Catching the Rhythm of Love* (Nashville: Thomas Nelson, 2000), pp. 102-03.

4. Richard Selzer, M.D., *Mortal Lessons: Notes in the Art of Surgery* (New York: Simon and Schuster, 1976), pp. 45-46.

5. Dr. Laura Schlessinger, *The Proper Care and Feeding of Marriage* (New York: HarperCollins, 2007), p. 127.

6. *Better Homes and Gardens,* October 2006, p. 258.

Chapter 11

1. James Dobson, *Love for a Lifetime* (Sisters, OR: Multnomah Publishers, 1987), p. 70.

2. *Time,* December 18, 2006, p. 123.

3. Cindy Sigler Dagnan, *The Chocolate Side of Life* (Webb City, MO: Covenant, 2003), p. 46.

About the Author

Cindy Sigler Dagnan has a passion for families: encouraging weary moms, cheering on desperate housewives, championing marriages in this age of disposable ones, making the most of the tender years in which God entrusts to us our little ones. She loves writing and speaking about those topics

If you would like to have Cindy speak or would like to schedule a marriage seminar with Cindy and her husband, Greg, you may contact her through her website www.cindydagnan.com.

~

Note from the Author

Precious readers, I would love to hear your stories, learn from your good ideas, and have the blessing of your feedback. You may contact me at cindydagnan@sbcglobal.net or through my website, www.cindydagnan.com.

Other Great Harvest House Reading

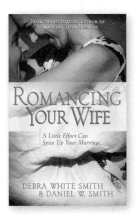

ROMANCING YOUR WIFE

by Debra White Smith and Daniel W. Smith

Do you want your husband to surprise you and put more romance in your relationship? *Romancing Your Wife* can help! Give this book to your hubby, and he'll discover ways to create an exciting, enthusiastic marriage.

Debra and her husband, Daniel, offer biblical wisdom and practical advice that when put into practice will help your husband mentally, emotionally, and physically improve his relationship with you. He'll discover tools to build a dynamite marriage, including how to—

- communicate his love more effectively
- make you feel cherished
- better understand your needs and wants
- create a unity of spirit and mind
- increase the passion in your marriage

From insights on little things that jazz up a marriage to more than 20 "Endearing Encounters," *Romancing Your Wife* sets the stage for love and romance.

RED-HOT MONOGAMY

Bill and Pam Farrel

With their trademark insight, humor, and candid personal perspectives, Bill and Pam Farrel reveal the truths about the sexual relationship in marriage and what husbands and wives need to know to keep the embers burning.

- *Sex is like fireworks!*—why a little skill turns marriage into red-hot monogamy
- How sex works best emotionally, physically, and physiologically
- How to avoid the pleasure thieves that steal your chance for fulfillment

The Farrels present difficult-to-discuss topics and biblical truths in universal language with sensitivity, fun, and understanding. This book inspires the gift of romance and passion to fuel your marriage with love!

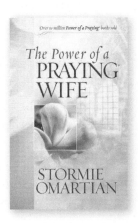

THE POWER OF A PRAYING® WIFE

Stormie Omartian

Bestselling author Stormie Omartian inspires you to develop a deeper relationship with your husband by praying for him and specific areas of his life including:

- decision-making
- family leadership
- spiritual strength

If you desire a closer relationship with your husband, you'll appreciate the life illustrations, select scripture verses, and the assurances of God's promises and power for your marriage.

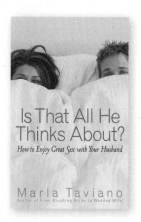

IS THAT ALL HE THINKS ABOUT?

Marla Taviano

For many married women, their sex life is a source of frustration instead of the pleasure they expected. Author Marla Taviano believes most women need an attitude adjustment before they and their husbands will experience a fulfilling sex life. With candor Marla helps you view sex God's way so you can:

- celebrate God's plan for women to be godly and sexual
- seek forgiveness for past sexual impurities and move on
- get creative, spice-up lovemaking, and increase desire

Marla debunks myths, calls women on their own issues, reveals the joy of sex, and presents hopeful advice that you will refer to again and again.